After a career in the private sector, government and Big 4 consulting the author Mark O'Connell established OCO Global in 2001. OCO Global has been an innovator and thought leader in the field of FDI since its inception, and has developed methodologies, databases and intelligence tools that have transformed our understanding of the FDI industry and led to several spin outs such as FDI Markets, Wavteq, and Eutopia. Today OCO employs 180 staff in 10 geographies, continues to set standards and is the go to advisor for government and companies seeking to optimize FDI impacts.

This book is aimed at students of FDI, practitioners in government and industry, funders, intermediaries and anyone who wants to understand what the fuss is all about.

AuthorHouse™ UK
1663 Liberty Drive
Bloomington, IN 47403 USA
www.authorhouse.co.uk
UK TFN: 0800 0148641 (Toll Free inside the UK)
UK Local: 02036 956322 (+44 20 3695 6322 from outside the UK)

ISBN: 979-8-8230-8917-3 (sc)
ISBN: 979-8-8230-8918-0 (e)

Library of Congress Control Number: 2024916197

Print information available on the last page.

Published by AuthorHouse 10/29/2024

authorHOUSE®

Contents

Preface

Most books I have come across on foreign direct investment (FDI) are written by academics and seek to make or disprove the macro-economic case for interventionalist FDI policies. Since most of the leading global economies are receptive to FDI and compete strongly to attract foreign companies, whilst developing countries regard FDI as a way of leapfrogging economic development, I have concluded that FDI is mostly a positive economic force for good.

I have worked all my career in advisory, government and private sector firms helping them to navigate international markets and negotiate with government. The insights I share in this book are from a practitioner's perspective. Much public sector money is wasted on ineffective FDI policies and practices, while the private sector is often naïve in its engagement with Government agencies and fails to maximize its leverage.

Equally FDI has changed substantively since I first became involved in the industry both in terms of which companies are actively investing, how they fund such investments, where these firms originate and how they invest, and the kinds of activities they locate overseas. There is also a much wider and plausible number of countries, regions and cities competing to win their investment.

I have observed that foreign capital and investment attraction is the policy lever of choice when nations experience an economic crisis, such as post-war rebuilding, the financial crisis of 2008, and more recently the global pandemic of 2019-2020. And this is because FDI delivers jobs, growth and positive headlines faster than major structural change, diversification of homegrown industries, or potentially unpopular fiscal measures.

To define my chosen career as a 'hustle' implies the industry is one big fraud or swindle. That would be unfair and inaccurate. I was inspired to call the book 'The Great FDI Hustle' by the glamourous Vegas heist movies where everyone is in on the con, the mob, the owners, the cops, and the politicians, and the suckers are the regular punters.

In the world of FDI the whiff of a swindle is never too far away in respect of the real motives behind an investment decision, was it truly mobile or contestable, did the government authorities need to intervene and if there were grants and incentives offered to the investor did they provide a good return on investment for the taxpayer, and what was in it for the middle men, consultants and advisors, not to mention the politician who needed a positive headline?

But whatever the methods, cross border investments have created millions of jobs across the world and have lifted countless countries, cities and regions out of economic doldrums and created wealth and prosperity with tangible and immediate impacts. So, while I encourage everyone to approach the subject of FDI and FDI attraction with a healthy measure of scepticism I truly believe the end justifies the means.

In the chapters that follow I will try to unpack the facts and fiction of the foreign direct investment business and share the fabulous journey that took myself and my firm into every kind of scrape and caper that made for 30 memorable years.

The book is aimed at students of FDI, people working in the industry either in government, advisory or private sector, and anyone else who wants to know what all the fuss is about.

CHAPTER 1

The Market Failure

Investment promotion, territorial marketing, business recruitment and retention, overseas direct investment: I wonder what the celebrated economist Adam Smith, whose core theory is that markets tend to work best when the government leaves them alone, would have made of it all? Yet in FDI attraction, we have created a government-led industry that does precisely the opposite!

If you are explaining, you are losing. For most of my career, I have tried to find a succinct way to describe what I do without seeing my audience glaze over, pitch me to manage their money, ask for stock tips, or sound like a snake-oil salesman. I'm still not sure I have nailed that, as my siblings and friends barely know what I do.

The truth is the average person does not know or care what FDI is, leaving aside the jargon. Foreign direct investment is a term dreamt up by economists and academics, and companies rarely describe themselves as foreign direct investors. And foreign direct investment means different things to different people.

Back in 2009, when Arnold Schwarzenegger was governor of California, I was invited to address an economic development audience from the various regions of the state and try to convince them of the merits of a state-wide policy to attract foreign investments. One part of the audience assumed I was talking about bringing foreign capital to rebuild the state's crumbling infrastructure. While others thought about international trade, many did not believe that such a large and economically powerful state needed to intervene, and the majority had a domestic view of attracting firms from other parts of the country. And since the event was held in Anaheim in the Disney resort, many delegates were more interested in what Mickey and his friends were up to than the economic challenges facing the state—of which there were (are) many!

As part of the pre-briefing for the conference, I was taken on a tour of the state capitol building in Sacramento, and I was shown to the governor's quarters, which had been tastefully decorated with art collected by his then wife, Maria Shriver. After a briefing from Dale Bonner, his secretary of commerce, I was shown to an internal garden that had a gazebo in the middle where Governor Schwarzenegger like to hold court and enjoy a cigar. Unfortunately for me, the main man was not at home that day, but I did get a souvenir personalized cigar.

I also learnt that every trade and investment mission that the governor led to Europe, Asia, and further afield was oversubscribed in terms of companies and investors because everyone wanted to hang out with Arnold on the governor's private jet and bask in the halo of autograph hunters and superfans everywhere he went. A dose of star power can work wonders when you want to meet the CEO of Volkswagen or Siemens on your tour of Germany! That left me wondering how my more mundane recommendations for practical FDI attraction strategies might measure up to the pulling power of the Terminator....

Most of the foreign firms that set up in California find their own way and never come into contact with the machinery of state or local government until it they have to file tax returns or apply for permits. And California (along with New York, which also has a very modest FDI attraction program) is consistently the number one or two state recipient of FDI volumes in the nation. So no market failure?

Figure 1.1: FDI Projects in the United States by State (December 2023)

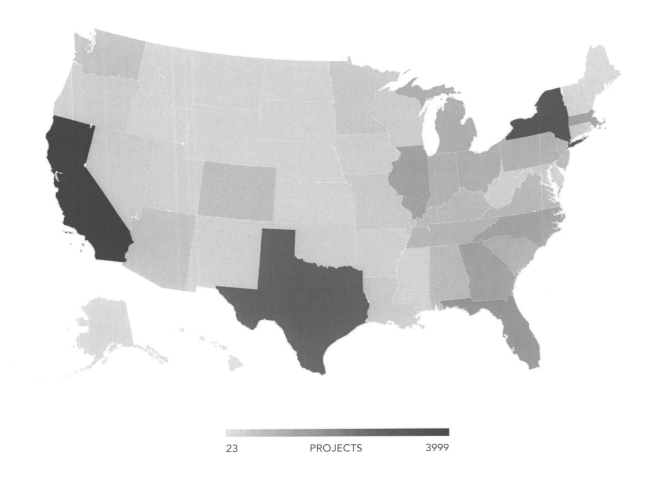

Destination State	Projects	Destination State	Projects	Destination State	Projects
California	3999	Kentucky	461	Delaware	119
New York	3148	Colorado	436	Oklahoma	118
Texas	2623	Washington	406	Iowa	107
Florida	1552	Arizona	392	West Virginia	103
Massachusetts	1168	Washington, DC	271	New Mexico	88
Georgia	1135	Maryland	265	New Hampshire	76
Illinois	1124	Wisconsin	243	Nebraska	63
North Carolina	1099	Missouri	232	Idaho	61
Michigan	902	Louisiana	223	North Dakota	57
Ohio	829	Minnesota	220	Maine	55
South Carolina	788	Nevada	213	Rhode Island	55
Pennsylvania	718	Connecticut	203	South Dakota	41
Indiana	676	Oregon	185	Hawaii	35
Tennessee	625	Kansas	149	Vermont	27
New Jersey	614	Mississippi	143	Alaska	24
Virginia	566	Utah	134	Montana	24
Alabama	502	Arkansas	121	Wyoming	23

Yes and no. The technology dominance of Silicon Valley where a concentration of talent, and the pervasiveness of VC and PE funding in the region, not to mention the sheer size of the internal market, means that aspiring tech firms are already aware of the offer, and their funders heavily influence their international expansion timing and locations. At the same time, there are many other options for ascendant tech firms that are less overheated than California, have more competitive skills, and offer better connectivity, lower taxes, and in some cases, incentives to new investors. Places like Phoenix, Austin, Denver, Vancouver, and Portland—if the West Coast is important—as well as Midwest locations such as Columbus, Minneapolis St Paul, and Chicago are also focused on tech and proactive in their attraction programs. Such places heavily promote their location and raise awareness of their offers domestically and internationally with target investors.

The large consulting firms do have economic development and site-selection practices, but these tend to be led by tax and incentivesadvisors, or real estate units that have a single agenda and do not always serve the wider needs of the investor, especially first-time investors who have multiple challenges and are a very important part of the market today. There is also a conflict and independence challenge at the heart of this engagement; fees contingent on incentives may not always drive the most impartial advice.

Within the large accountancy firms, the audit practice that owns the relationship with the corporate HQ must remain independent of the advisory business and is reluctant to share intelligence or engage with other parts of the practice. I saw this first-hand during my time with PwC and more lately as a contractor to EY. Financial independence rules, if anything, have become even stricter, and it is difficult for the Big 4 and tier-two firms to really deliver on the theoretical advantage of their global footprint.

On the client side, today, the biggest volumes in FDI come from early stage young technology and business services firms or companies from emerging markets. They are rarely household names, unlike multinational companies such as GE, Siemens, and Microsoft that dominated the FDI landscape until the start of this century. These large established corporates have internal real estate and government relations people who are in a permanent cycle of site selection, rationalization, and optimization and know the economic and political power their decisions can leverage. This shift in FDI reflects changing consumer trends and business models. At the start of the century, the top three investors in Western Europe were IBM, Siemens, and Microsoft, but more recently, these have been replaced by Amazon and logistics companies Deutsche Post and La Poste on the wave of ecommerce trends.

So much of today's FDI demand comes from startups and scaleups that are often funded by VC/PE and are in a hurry to internationalize and grab market share to raise their valuations. They have little or no experience of in investing overseas and limited bandwidth to make a proper assessment. Consequently and often they rely on external advisors, including investment promotion agencies (IPAs) and economic development organizations (EDOs) to help navigate their expansion optionsprocess.

Unfortunately, many of the most successful and longest established IPAs around the world are still mandated politically and organized and measured internally to capture FDI from large corporates with the promise of jobs, capital investment, and spillover effects and tend to neglect the nimble services and tech startups that are the investors of today and tomorrow.

In a way, it is understandable as analysis of the data from the last five years showed that although new tech startups account for around 25 per cent of all new projects, they only provide 14 per cent of jobs and 15 per cent of investment. [1]But this misses the growth potential of startups. For example, Berlin-based fashion e-commerce company Zalando grew to become the tenth biggest employer in the city over the last twelve years, while North of England-based Challenge-trg Group became one of the United Kingdom's fastest-growing startups in 2021 when it expanded from 260 employees to more than a thousand in two years.

Progressive cities such as Berlin, Stockholm, and Denver are alive to this opportunity and have been able to pivot their offer and approach to resonate.

---

[1]There is no exact data on start-up FDI, so this estimate is based on a comparison of new greenfield FDI in the software and IT sector from companies with revenue above and below $30m.

[2]All figures related to FDI projects, investments, and capital investments are taken from the Financial Times's fDi Markets database unless otherwise stated in the text.

Meanwhile, many global cities are enslaved by big real estate bets on the future of global corporations. Think Canary Wharf in London, La Defence in Paris, Battery Park in New York— albeit they are playing in new product offers like Tech City in London and Station 17 in Paris to counter the demand from startups. The remote working and hybrid models that evolved during the pandemic era are also likely to influence how cities evolve their real estate offer.

In the last fifteen years since Jim O'Neill, then chairman of Goldman Sachs, successfully coined the phrase BRICS to describe ascendant economies of Brazil, Russia, India, China, and South Africa, we have also witnessed significant growth in outbound FDI from these markets. Since 2003, India and China have doubled their outward FDI from 3 to 6 per cent of global investment, while the United States has been going in the opposite direction from 25 per cent of all FDI to 20 per cent by 2021.[2]

Each nation takes a very different approach, with China outbound investment more state controlled though its state-owned enterprises (SOEs) that need a license to trade outside China, while India is more large family conglomerates and entrepreneurial leddriven. Companies from these and other emerging markets such as Latin America tend to be well capitalized, privately owned, and in a hurry. Their approach to international expansion tends to be through acquisition of well-known brands and technologies rather than conventional greenfield FDI. Despite the huge success and local economic development impact of emerging market acquisitions of western companies, such as Geely's acquisition of Volvo, most Western Hemisphere IPAs are not mandated or equipped to deal with M&A and in some cases are suspicious or protectionist of this type of investment, assuming it will be a land or asset grab and lead to job losses and consolidation.

The trend to introduce policy to protect national industries or ensure self-sufficiency has been accelerated by the rising influence of China on world trade; the election of populist leaders in the United States, Latin America, and parts of Europe; and the pandemic, which has reawakened mercantilist ideologies. There was a time when protectionism was confined mainly to defense and energy; now it extends to food, medical equipment, and data, which covers practically every industry today from fintech to heath-tech. Consequently, we can expect foreign investors to face much more scrutiny and the job of investment attraction to become much harder.

According to Dr Mike Short, the chief scientific advisor to the Department of Business and Trade in the United Kingdom, the global pandemic of 2020 has accelerated the adoption of technology by government, business, and citizens by five years, and it will change irreversibly the future of work: where we work, who we work for, and how we work. This, perhaps more than any of the other challenges outlined above, will transform the future of FDI, which will no longer be about real estate or even location but access to skills, technology, progressive regulation, and market access.

For the last twenty years, OCO has operated in the white space we call the FDI market failure—where private-sector clients don't understand government, government doesn't know how to engage with the private sector, and the intermediaries are conflicted or priced out of the game. Meanwhile, technology has become the biggest disrupter of all.

In a world where most majority of developed economies can provide a stable business environment; protection for foreign-owned assets; access to skills and facilities; reliable infrastructure; and competitive costs (coincidentally, all the FDI promotional literature makes the same claims), only those locations that can truly differentiate their offer through specialization (Denmark offshore wind), strategic geographic advantage (Dubai, Miami and Singapore for logistics/gateway), unique incentives or cost advantages (Canada and New Zealand for film production), and most importantly of all, the availability of relevant skills/workforce that match the investor needs (Lisbon games software engineers, Florida space tech) are likely to succeed in a fast- changing world.

When I began my career in FDI thirty years ago, the majority of my advisory colleagues and those working for government in investment promotion had a background in real estate, urban planning, or tax. Today, technology and vertical industry experience is far more common, alongside financial modelling and data analysis/comparison skills.

In summary, the FDI advisory and attraction business has become far more complex, specialized, and competitive than what was once essentially a real estate and incentives game serving large multinationals.

CHAPTER 2

The Romance of FDI

Mirror, mirror, on the wall: Who's the fairest of them all? Like in the fairytale Snow White , nations involved in promoting FDI are prone to self-delusion about the attractiveness of the location, often amplified by an echo chamber of politically motivated advisors.

Securing foreign investment and the associated jobs is widely regarded by governments as the most impactful and flattering of all economic successes. It demonstrates the effectiveness of government policies to create an attractive and competitive business environment and brings valuable political capital to those administrations behind the policy.

Figure 2.1: The FDI Photo Opp!

Think of President Macron's charm offensive to Global Tech in no less of a romantic setting than the Palace of Versailles ahead of the 2018 Davos Summit. Or Barak Obama's triumphant rallying at the SelectUSA Investment Summit where all fifty states lay on the red carpet for foreign investor delegates. Or David Cameron's leverage of the London 2012 Games to showcase UK capabilities to VIP investors. Be in no doubt: FDI is big business and highly politically motivated. Not unlike the star-pulling power of the Schwarzenegger governor missions, many CEOs are flattered and seduced by the allure of palaces, hanging out with presidents, and the access that money cannot buy—or perhaps their investment decisions can…

Attracting FDI is also highly competitive, and countries, regions, and cities fight to position themselves in the minds of investors to secure mobile and contestable projects. Annual league tables from EY, IBM, and FT are eagerly awaited to assess performance and determine who is on the podium for the most attractive state, nation, or city in the eyes of foreign investors on the basis of how many FDI projects they attracted.

It is easy to be seduced by the industry. During my leadership at OCO, my firm has been appointed by ambitious and ascendant countries and regions to advise and formulate their FDI strategies based on our track record and success in delivering FDI programs in developed countries like the United Kingdom, France, and Italy, as well as numerous US states. Examples that have stayed with me include the following case studies.

Case Study 1

In Costa Rica, OCO worked for CINDE the national investment agency on their life sciences/med-tech attraction strategy where they aspired to achieve the same FDI success as Ireland a country with a similar population with limited natural resources but a big emphasis on education and skilled workers.

CINDE had developed a number of specialized med tech focused business parks within their free zone areas with sterilization facilities and clean rooms to offer turnkey facilities to US firms looking to establish an America's hub to serve central and south America. I recall being in the Baxter facility where the productivity data for each of their global sites was presented in the reception area and the Costa Rica facility topped the league of performance which speaks to the internal competition within corporates to maintain and expand country footprints.

The agency was extremely motivated to ensure that our project manager and I saw the complete strength and depth of the med tech cluster in Costa Rica. We experienced 12 hour days with 8-10 meetings across the country led by a very attractive and highly intelligent sector lead from the agency. By the end of the 4 day program, I understood clearly how investors could be seduced by the offer in this warm, friendly and biologically diverse country.

The life sciences sector in Costa Rica now employs more than twenty-two thousand people and is worth $3.7bn in exports. Today, the country hosts seventy-two med-tech multinationals, including thirteen of the top twenty OEMs, with investment promotion agency CINDE posting a record year in 2020.[3]

[3]Information on Costa Rica is taken from the investment promotion agency, CINDE (https://www.cinde.org/en), and The Central America Group, Life Sciences in Costa Rica, 2019 (http://www.thecentralamericangroup.com/life-sciences-in-costa-rica/).

Case Study 2

A longstanding client, and the first US state to engage OCO to represent them internationally in 2005, is Enterprise Florida.

At the time, Jeb Bush was Florida state governor, and he had the vision to reposition the state as a serious business, technology, and innovation location, building on its well-established allure for tourism, sunshine, and citrus fruit. OCO won a contract to represent Florida in a number of EU markets and help them engage with European firms to build a pipeline of investment projects. So far so good. On my first familiarization visit to the State, I met with Enterprise Florida leadership and was introduced to their board by the CEO Darrell Kelley as their newly appointed 'big game hunter'. Talk about creating an expectation and vision of a wall full of trophies. 'Indiana Jones O'Connell' to the rescue!

Happily, for me and my firm, Florida is a great place to do business and a gateway to the Americas; our partnership with Enterprise Florida has brought more than $1bn of investment and created more than thirty thousand jobs in the last fifteen years. This includes companies of the stature of Safran in Aerospace, Greencore in food, and Lloyd's of London in finance, alongside the new breed of tech unicorns such as Wise PLC (formerly TransferWise) and Exscientia.

During this time, Florida has been governed by mostly center-right administrations, starting with Jeb Bush (1999–2007), and then Charlie Crist (2007–2011), Rick Scott (2011–2019), and currently Ron DeSantis. Bush was governor at a time of plenty apart from the mixed reviews of his brother George W Bush as President for leading the nation into the Iraq war and the negative impact that had on US foreign policy/reputation in Europe. I recall having to shuttle him and his delegation though the side door of the Conrad Hotel in Dublin to avoid the anti-American protests at the front door. The romance of international trade and FDI was not lost on Charlie Crist, who enjoyed numerous international missions to Latin America and Europe; but unlike his predecessor, he had limited interest/experience in business and was out of his depth in investor meetings but a smooth political operator who has since reinvented himself several times.

Governor Scott inherited a difficult economic cycle after the financial crisis, which hit Florida hard and unemployment was in double figures due to the subprime mortgage market collapse and the drop in tourism and leisure spending. He memorably pledged to create seven hundred thousand jobs in seven years if he was given two terms. He was and he did, and foreign investment played a significant part in Florida's recovery.

It's early days for Ron DeSantis, and the pandemic curbed international travel and engagement with foreign investment, but in an outward looking and multicultural melting pot like Florida, no politician can afford to ignore the Latino vote and the impact that Americas' intertrade and investment dependencies have on the prosperity of the state. It has also been inspiring to witness the exodus of major tech CEOs from the overheated West Coast and major hedge funds relocating to Miami's 'Silicon Beach' to experience remote working in a very attractive and lightly regulated location.

Case Study 3

Lastly, a more obscure but equally memorable engagement that speaks to the romance of FDI was in Russia in 2010 working for the city of Tomsk in western Siberia. Until Glasnost, Tomsk was not on any map. It was a secret city isolated in the frozen Urals, a five-hour flight from Moscow. This city was home to several elite research and university institutions where the Soviets carried out their atomic research programs, shrouded in secrecy and cold war sensitivity. My mission was to understand more about their offer and determine how it could be presented to foreign investors.

An investment proposition around the best scientific minds in Russia, all in one place and available at incredibly low cost was not such a hard sell. However, changing Russian mindsets from a centrally planned model to one where you need to understand the market and competitors, differentiate your offer, and sell yourself was a much bigger cultural challenge. After one week amongst these reserved but genuine people, I was being hailed as a prophet and soothsayer!

After my week of training and capacity building, the leader of the investment agency lifted me off my feet and gave me a bearhug, tears of gratitude streaming down his cheeks, and insisted I come to a celebration banquet in my honour. This was to be my first initiation into Russian business hospitality and trust me when I tell you it is not for the fainthearted. I was driven in deep snow to a rustic lodge restaurant in a forest on the outskirts of Tomsk to be greeted by a formidable, stuffed, seven-feet tall Russian bear attending to the entrance.

Once inside, in a private room, a roaring log fire crackled in the hearth while an impressive candlelit banquet table was laid out for around sixteen diners. After some formalities about where the honoured guests should be seated and by whom, I and my Russian colleague, Julia, took our places. Drinks were poured (vodka or brandy were the only choices in shot glasses), washed down with cranberry juice chasers (the Tomsk region is one of the largest producers of cranberries, as well as enriched uranium). And so began the first of multiple toasts, to FDI, to the president, to mother Russia, to Ireland (in my honour), to prosperity, to health, and to happiness. It was open mike, and one or other of the participants stood up every ten or fifteen minutes to propose a new toast, whereupon we all stood, raised a glass, and downed another shot. I really lost count, and even the interesting food—frozen whitefish cubes seasoned with chili flakes, eaten frozen and crunchy, smoked reindeer meat, borscht soup, and pelmeni— could not counter the effects of neat, ice-cold vodka.

As an influencer of investment into this remote place, my lasting impression was the warmth and genuine curiosity of the people I met. I came away with a determination to do everything I could to advocate the location as a fun place to visit, invest in, and enjoy.

In the developed world, investment promotion has been around in one form or another for sixty to seventy years, ever since the forces of globalization encouraged multinational firms to expand internationally and leverage cost efficiencies, skills, raw materials and market access. One of the earliest pure play investment promotion agencies (IPA) was IDA Ireland, founded in 1949 and borne out of the necessity to drag Ireland out of a low productivity, low GDP, protectionist economy highly dependent on the United Kingdom. IDA Ireland used incentives, especially industrial sites, low corporate taxes and a laser focus on meeting the needs of the mostly US corporate investor, whether that be provision of skills, R&D facilities and supports, access to government departments and a media fueled hero's welcome for the foreign investor.

Today FDI continues to drive the economy with IDA Ireland clients accounting for 11 per cent of total national employment and expenditure reaching €38.5bn in 2022, a 13.4 per cent year-on-year increase and the highest level of expenditure on record[4]. In 2019, the stock of FDI in Ireland exceeded €1 trillion for the first time[5] and by 2022 it was equal to 264 per cent of Ireland's GDP. Ireland comfortably outperforms similar sized economies such as Belgium and Sweden, who's FDI as a share of GDP in 2022 was 91 per cent and 65 per cent respectively[6].

IDA is recognized amongst peers and emerging countries as a best-in-class example of an IPA. But there is romance in this story too…

Apart from being a highly disciplined, sector-focused organization with a major emphasis on aftercare— looking after existing clients so they continue to expand and bring their supply chains—IDA Ireland also achieved its success by playing to the gallery. In the early days, they identified C suite executives in major US corporations with Irish ancestry, even without LinkedIn and social media. This was not so difficult due to surnames like Murphy, O'Brien, and Fitzgerald, through the tightly knit Irish American communities, especially those on the Eastern seaboard in places like Boston and Philadelphia and IDA appealed to a subconscious yearning to do something for the 'oul' country.

Of course, FDI decisions are risky and must be rooted in solid commercial planning, not emotion, and IDA would not have been successful without a convincing investment proposition. However, in a location beauty parade, where the competition is more or less evenly matched, the emotional card trumps all, and investors do think about intangibles, such as visiting with their families, playing golf, exploring historical links, and a halo effect that an investment that is perceived to be giving something back will deliver for their personal and corporate reputations. It is no accident that significant foreign investors are often greeted on the steps of their arriving flights by senior ministers of state, or in some cases the Taoiseach himself. That's Ireland's commitment to FDI attraction.

Some years back I attended an annual medical devices trade event in Los Angeles (on behalf of CINDE Costa Rica, who I mentioned earlier) to pitch the location as an FDI option. In the center of the exhibition hall was a double-height booth hosted by IDA Ireland. Downstairs they had images of the Irish operations of the largest US medical-device firms in the world— companies such as Baxter, Abbott, and Medtronic, who all had successful manufacturing operations in Ireland. Upstairs was a packed VIP bar serving draft Guinness. I engaged one of the IDA representatives close to the booth and asked him why he was not out working the floor. He told me they already have ten out of the top twelve med-tech firms in the world, and they were focused on aftercare and embedding, not new business. He then added that any US medical-device firm proposing an overseas expansion to their board needed to explain why, if Ireland was not on the list of shortlisted location options. Focusing narrowly on one market and specialism—in this case US med-tech manufacturing, attractive sites, skills, and market access, along with one of the lowest corporate tax rates in Europe (throw in a bit of romance and links golf for good measure)—conveys why Ireland has achieved a dominant and unshakable market position.

I often observe that for every dollar governments spend on FDI attraction, they will spend at least ten times that budget on trade/export promotion. This is because exporters and local enterprise are

---

[4]IDA Ireland Annual Report, 2023 (https://www.idaireland.com/annual-reports/ida-ireland-annual-Central [5]Statistics Office, Foreign Direct Investment Annual, 2019 (https://www.cso.ie/en/releasesandpublications/er/fdi/foreigndirectinvestmentannual2019).

[6]OECD, FDI in Stocks, 2022 (https://www.oecd.org/en/data/indicators/fdi-stocks.html).

constituents and vote for governments, and there are more of them, even if their impact through export earnings on economic development is rarely ten parts of the foreign investor. The fact is foreign investors tend to be larger, more established players and will create more jobs faster than a bloom of local enterprises or first-time exporters. While government ministers do like to champion exporters and spearhead trade missions and international outreach, the junket accusation is ever present and the economic impact takes much longer to measure, by which time they could be out of office. FDI, on the other hand, brings more immediate and high impact results, including exports in many cases, and you don't have to leave home—except perhaps to visit the constituency and cut the ribbon on the new FDI plant.

Going back to our friends in Florida, research in 2015 from the Office of Economic and Demographic Research found that the Export Assistance Program had a return on investment (ROI) for the state of 1.85, while the International Offices Program to attract foreign investors had a return of 3.98. For every dollar spent on international offices, the state received three dollars and ninety-eight cents back in tax revenue.[7]

In some countries, exports and FDI attraction are housed in the same organization, mostly to the detrimental performance of both, as the client, activity, and skillsets are different. However, when you see colleagues from both divisions working side by side, it is obvious that the FDI team consider themselves the smartest guys in the room, and their jobs and careers are the most coveted internally. Here again this is because the community at large and internal stakeholders see FDI as the sexy and most valuable part of the operation. FDI promotion is highly competitive, and the client (investor) has options and needs to be sold, while trade/export promotion is a captive and often transactional volume business, so relationships between agency and client can be transient. Whereas landing a foreign investor takes time and multiple touch points, and once landed there are critical and long-term relationship or account management requirements. So again, another chance for romance.

In North America, and to a lesser and more regulated extent Europe and Asia, corporate location decisions are often supported by intermediaries called site selectors. Many come from real estate and tax backgrounds and work for private-sector clients to help them navigate options and negotiate with economic developers the most suitable locations for their expansion projects. In North America, site selector fees are often contingent on the size of the incentives package that is negotiated with a community. There is an inherent conflict and independence/objectivity challenge at the heart of this business model that would be considered anticompetitive in Europe.

For as long as US states (and Canadian provinces) compete with each other and are willing to write cheques to support big investments, site selectors (and their corporate clients) will be able to shop their projects around to the highest bidder.

I have seen firsthand the bonfire of the vanities at economic development conferences, such as IEDC in the United States or Cornet and MIPIM in Europe. The site-selection consultants are feted and lionized by the economic development community, who crave their attention and solicit their advice on how to get on shortlists and be considered for future projects. There are all-expenses-paid, lavish corporate hospitality events involving sport, entertainment, fine dining, and helicopter tours to curry favor and get on the radar of site selectors. This is a particular US phenomenon, and usually connected with intrastate competition for projects from US corporates, where fees are connected to incentives; while in Europe and elsewhere, fees are paid by the corporate and unrelated to the size of the incentives package, which is regulated by EU anticompetition rules. Many EU and international investors in the United States do not realize their buying power and could potentially attract higher incentives to underwrite their investment if location is flexible.

A high-profile example from 2018 was the announcement by Amazon that they were on the lookout for a second North American HQ. They bypassed the site selector community and went direct to the economic developers representing

[7]Florida Office of Economic and Demographic Research, Return-on-Investment for International Trade and Business Development Programs, 2015 (http://www.edr.state.fl.us/Content/returnoninvestment/ROI-IntTradeandBusinessDevProg.pdf).

hundreds of communities in the United States and Canada, setting out their requirements in a tender specification. Millions of tax dollars were spent by economic development organizations, often with the support of site-selection consultants to respond and demonstrate to Amazon their unconditional love and support for their investment. Some communities went to unprecedented lengths and renamed rivers and babies after the company to gain attention and make the shortlist.

Amazon's request for proposals stated that cities should think big, which was certainly true in one area: incentives. Maryland's offer of $8.5bn in tax and infrastructure incentives was believed to be the biggest, while the original winner, New York, was estimated to have offered $3.5bn. North Carolina even passed new legislation that increased the amount of income taxes that would be rebated to Amazon, a practice that Good Jobs First, a corporate accountability advocacy group, called 'paying taxes to your boss'.

Nobody knows for sure how much this bidding ended up costing each city, but 238 bids were submitted, and a tight six-week deadline will have occupied a big chunk of economic development time and resources, only for Amazon to pause the project in 2023 in light of job losses across the industry.[8]

I believe the whole competition was a politically motivated stunt. Amazon have more up-to-date and relevant data on location comparatives than the best and most experienced corporate location advisor, thanks to their dominant position on web services, ecommerce, and logistics. They were always going to pick an East Coast capital with a concentration of suppliers and buyers like New York. One of my favorite schadenfreude moments of my career is when the community of Long Island, New York, rose up against their decision and rejected them as a threat to their business community, an exploiter of labor, and a tax avoider. History and the more recent pandemic have shown that the instincts of the good people of Long Island were right.

Amazon is far from a force for good and has a reductive effect on economic development, closing high streets, automating warehousing, and monopolizing sectors where they can control supply and demand and pricing. A study by the Bank of Canada found that that Amazon's product expansion accounted for 37 per cent of the observed reduction in product scope of Canadian online retailers.[9]

A more uplifting and contemporary example, but also one that exposes the vainglorious attempts of national governments to demonstrate their virility in attracting high-profile FDI, was the competition for Tesla's European gigafactory for their next-generation electric cars. OCO worked closely with the Italian government to prepare their pitch while we are aware that the French were being advised by McKinsey and the British and Dutch by other advisors. The national pride amongst giants of the automotive sector, such as France, Italy, Germany, and the United Kingdom explains the lengths they were prepared to go to in order to secure the project with the close involvement of prime ministers and senior government ministers. In the end, the project went to Berlin, an unlikely place for automotive manufacturing, with limited supply chains compared to Stuttgart as a German option, or Midlands United Kingdom, or Turin as the home of Italian automotive. However, the result speaks loudly to the fact that Tesla consider themselves a tech startup rather than a traditional automotive company, and Berlin is the epitome of cool in the European tech start scene, and there happened to be a large disused VW site ready to go with no planning hassles.

I hope I have demonstrated that for political leaders, economic developers, intermediaries, and their private sector clients, there is a romance and heady courtship at the heart of every FDI deal. And for the losers: there is heartbreak, humiliation, and the damage to political capital. It is telling that few economies track or publish information on lost FDI deals or disinvestment.

---

[8]For a full account of the Amazon HQ saga, there is are interesting articles in the Washington Post (www.washingtonpost.com/technology/2018/11/13/winners-losers-amazons-hq-decision/) and the *New Statesman* (www.newstatesman.com/culture/2019/06/the-hunger-games-for-cities-inside-the-amazon-hq2-bid-process).

[9]Bank of Canada staff working paper, Amazon Effects in Canadian Online Retail Firm-Product-Level Data, 2019 (https://www.bankofcanada.ca/2019/10/staff-working-paper-2019-42/).

CHAPTER 3

The Politics of FDI

In the early noughties the place to be every June for politicians, FDI professionals, government agencies, and major investors was at the beach in La Baule on the West Atlantic Coast of France. The annual investment conference was highly influential and attracted marquee speakers of the heft of GE boss Jeff Immelt, Klaus Kleinfeld of Siemens, and leading politicians such as Thierry le Breton and Christine Lagarde. The glamour of the occasion by the Barriere Casino in the splendid surroundings of La Baule les Pins attracted the celebrities of the industry and was a think-tank for new approaches, investor perspectives, and innovation. It was also an opportunity to keep France on the world stage as a key location for FDI, with the event costs underwritten by EY and the Regional Development Agency Ouest Atlantique.

OCO was responsible for the program of Texas governor Rick Perry when he visited the conference in 2008 as a keynote speaker. Governor Perry travelled with his extended family and entourage, and it was difficult to keep them all to the tight agenda of the conference. He memorably kept Christiane Lagarde waiting onstage in the main conference hall for several uncomfortable minutes before showing up late in a Western-style suit, Stetson hat, and boots. When Madame Lagarde enquired icily if he was ready, he tilted his hat at her and said, "Yes, ma'am; I was born ready," and winked at the audience. This display of arrogance was further compounded when instead of talking about Texas engagement with green energy technologies and cooperation with European firms as he was billed to do, he went off on a solo run about the great state of Texas and how he wanted to reduce government interference and red tape that stood between Texas and the American Dream. It was a stark reminder of the intersection of politics and FDI and the impact that policies can have on the attractiveness of nations to different sectors and source markets.

While I was on secondment to the UKTI, now the Department for Business and Trade between 2011 and 2012 as interim head of Investment, I got an irate email from one of the special advisors (SPADs) to David Cameron's recently elected coalition government. The email asserted that during a recent garden party in the prime minister's constituency, a disgruntled investor from South Africa in the artificial diamonds/cubic zirconia sector mentioned he was not happy with the response and engagement levels of the agency and could I look into the case. I sensed danger because this was the same SPAD who had played a part in the conception of Tech City in London and the revival of the Old Street roundabout, now called Silicon roundabout. He believed that UKTI was a total waste of space and that he could run the entire investment attraction efforts from his BlackBerry as the future was all digital and virtual.

When I dug into the background of the case, I discovered the investor was proposing a small, low-value footprint operation with few jobs and limited capital, motivated by access to UK markets and the investor's personal circumstances—a couple of sons in UK education and likely to be coming more regularly to the country. I offered to meet the SPAD and explain how the opportunity had been triaged and tagged as low value by our investment team, and we had responded to all the questions promptly and connected him with the local authority representatives who could have supported and facilitated his investment.

I was invited to 10 Downing Street to respond to the challenge within a day or two and presented myself at the reception. The SPAD came down to meet me and was disarmingly charming and welcoming (aren't they always?). He took me on a brief tour of the building before settling us down in a waiting area beside the cabinet office. What struck me was the limited attention and bandwidth of the guy, who seemed constantly distracted by his BlackBerry and anxious to get on to the next thing. I took him calmly though the case, offered to describe how we prioritize investment support in the team. I explained our services and success in winning investments for the United Kingdom using examples of better high-profile investments that created jobs, technology, and positive headlines across the country, which seemed to get his attention. It made me realize that the politicians and their advisors have limited knowledge or understanding of what actually happens operationally in large swathes of the civil service and are only attuned to the political impact where it provides a halo on their particular policies and campaigns.

Fortunately, FDI has the power to create ribbon cutting and 'hero' moments for politicians in front of the media cameras, and during the planning for the London 2012 Games there was enormous pressure on the department to serve up regular and appetizing news stories about positive investment decisions to coincide with the program of investor set pieces and events around the Games themselves.

Incredibly, for such a high profile and politically sensitive activity such as foreign investment attraction, when OCO established in 2001 there was very little economic evidence to assess performance of countries and sectors over and above FDI stocks and flows and balance of payments data, which is only available at a national level and often creates a misleading picture when it is skewed by a tax-avoiding special-purpose vehicles (SPVs) in countries like Cayman Islands or Panama or a major M&A deal, amplifying or reducing the balance of FDI stock. For example, Belgium's outbound flows receive a regular boost from brewing giant InBev, which paid

$52bn for Anheuser-Busch in 2008 and $79bn for SABMiller in 2016.

From the very beginning, to advise regions or companies on FDI strategies, I felt it was critical for OCO to develop an empirical base to track the FDI data at a project level so we could understand which countries were the main donors and recipients, which sectors and activities were generating mobile

contestable projects, and most importantly which companies were behind these deals.

What began as a university PhD project by one of my former colleagues, Dr Henry Loewendahl, trying to collate an aggregate picture of project announcements by companies in the media and though their annual reports, as well as announcements from the regions who won the investments, this Excel spreadsheet evolved to become the leading source of FDI trends and insights and is today owned by the Financial Times (FT). FDi Markets database was originally developed in 2003 by OCO as an online subscription database until it was acquired by Pearson Group in 2008, who owned the Financial Times at the time. Greenfield and expansion announcements by corporates in this dataset go back as far as 2003, and depending on the year and economic cycle number, as few as fifteen thousand and as many as twenty thousand projects can be analysed by source market, region, and city as well as destination, sector, activity, and motives down to individual company level.

Those numbers in themselves tell a story since amongst these project announcements, up to a quarter could be expansions of existing footprints (so not as contestable), and around half will be resource or market-seeking investments (such as mining or sales offices), which are also not genuinely mobile or contestable. So, the real pool of demand is perhaps as few as 6000-7000 projects a year. Yet there are an estimated ten thousand economic-development organizations or IPAs around the world competing for this narrow pool of projects, which feels like an excessive amount of resources and effort for a relatively narrow prize. Ahh, but then there is the politics of it all... so risk-reward relationship goes out the window.

Today there are other sources that use the same methodology and track the same information, notably from IBM and the EY Attractiveness Survey, but OCO can genuinely claim to be a pioneer in the industry, and our embrace of a data-driven approach to FDI advisory was and remains a key differentiator in our approach.

A big contributor to OCO's success throughout the noughties and, in spite of being a small firm with limited marketing resources, was our access to this unique intelligence on FDI. When we released trends and analysis of FDI flows, the data was regularly cited and referenced by international organizations such as UNCTAD and OECD and quoted in influential periodicals such as Financial Times , Wall Street Journal, and The Economist. Even if purists could pick holes in our methodology in capturing the data, the fact that it was a global dataset being updated daily, and that we had a real company name behind each record rather than an abstract aggregate statistic, brought the trends to life and comforted our investment promotion agency (IPA) clients that their work and involvement was being recognized.

After the sale of fDi Markets to FT in 2008, OCO continues to subscribe to the data and use it in many of its consulting engagements. Since 2018, OCO has been working closely with EY to research and produce their European Investment Monitor (EIM) database, which feeds their EY Attractiveness Report, using the strength of our IPA networks and contacts to share and validate their investment performances. The political attention that this modest and highly technical report receives each May, when it is published, is extraordinary and speaks to the acute sense of competition amongst European nations to be the most attractive and top of the leader board in the FDI stakes. United Kingdom, France and Germany have been top three for as long as there are records, but lately, thanks to Brexit, the UK crown has been snatched by France, and Germany is stealthily gaining market share too alongside Spain, while smaller challenger nations such as Ireland, Netherlands, Belgium, and Portugal punch above their weight. It's like a judgment on their government's performance.

Table 3.1 Leading Countries for FDI as Ranked by the European Investment Monitor (2017–22)

Country	2017	2018	2019	2020	2021	2022
UK	1	1	2	2	2	2
Germany	2	3	3	3	3	3
France	3	2	1	1	1	1
Netherlands	4	8	6	8	11	11
Russia	5	9	8	11	NA	NA
Spain	6	4	4	4	4	4
Turkey	7	7	10	7	5	5
Belgium	8	5	5	5	6	9
Poland	9	6	7	6	9	8
Ireland	10	10	8	9	10	10
Portugal	17	17	11	10	8	6
Italy	19	14	12	12	7	7

Source: EY, European Investment Monitor (2017–22) (https://www.ey.com/en_gl/foreign-direct-investment-surveys)

During the lifetime of OCO we have experienced three significant global economic shocks, beginning with the bursting of the tech-stock bubble, which took place when we first established in 2001, followed by the financial crash of 2008–10, and more recentlynow, more lately, the global pandemic. We can also add some regional sideshows, such as the ascendancy of China, the Latin American economies' rise and falter, the engagement and retreat of Russia in the global economy, Arab Spring, Trump Populism, and more recentlylately, the rise of Africa, and the isolation of post-Brexit United Kingdom within Europe.

At the time of writing, the Russian 'military exercises' (sic), aka war in Ukraine, are destabilising confidence in energy and food security, disrupting supply chains, and risks wider regional escalation pitting NATO against Russia (and by proxy China) and undermining global investor confidence.

Figure 3.1: Global FDI and M&A Activities (1980–2020)

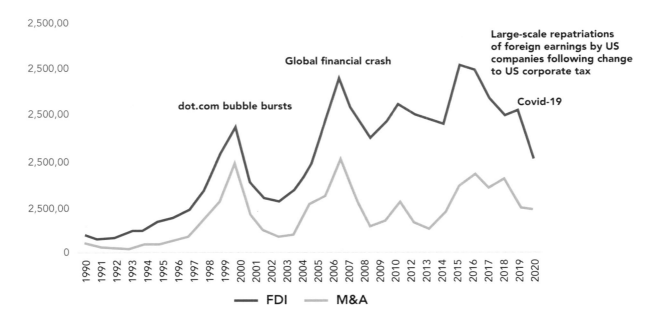

Source: Financial Times, fDi Markets database (https://www.fdimarkets.com/)

FDI flows are closely aligned with M&A volumes globally, and one tends to track the other, as the graph above illustrates. One of the attractions of FDI is to help insulate companies from exposure and crisis in one location and allow them to mitigate supply and market upheaval on a more global basis.

As an advisor and partner to many economic-development organizations around the world, I have observed that we tend to do better in a crisis than a boom when a rising tide lifts all boats. By their very nature government agencies are not as nimble or agile as the private sector, and during periods of economic challenges with rising company failures and job losses, FDI attraction can be regarded as a silver bullet to rapidly kickstart the economy.

For example, one of the first projects OCO was involved in came about thanks to the closure of leading automotive manufacturer Rover Group in the British Midlands. The local agencies put together a program called The Rover Task Force, which was mandated to mitigate the damage to the local economy by finding alterative jobs for the redundant workers, retaining and promoting the site and capabilities to new investors. OCO undertook an audit of companies and skills in the region as part of a wider new investment proposition.

To our surprise (and the surprise of the stakeholders in Coventry, Solihull, and Warwickshire), there was a vibrant cluster of some twelve hundred technology firms and some twenty-thousand skilled workers active between the three authorities. We repositioned the offer as a transport technologies proposition and branded the region as a 'software triangle', as it was technologically intensive and heavily export and supply chain integrated. Throughout the next decade the Midlands and the United Kingdom as a whole went on to recover the glory days of the 1970s when Britain was a global powerhouse in the sector. By 2013, Britain was again producing almost 1.5 million cars a year and employing close to one million workers in high-value jobs. And then along came Brexit and ruined the party... in 2022, Britain produced only seven hundred thousand cars.

OCO European offices in Frankfurt and Paris regularly engage with regions that are poised to lose a large OEM investor due to rationalization or consolidation, putting jobs and economic prosperity at risk. Unlike North America and the United Kingdom, there is legislation in place to encourage the exiting investor to support efforts to find a replacement tenant, or repurpose the facilities and staff by using incentives, retraining, and compensation, not just redundancy. This has proven positive for firms such as Siemens, Bosch, and Ford; when they close a plant, they must minimize the brand and reputational damage by helping mitigate the economic pain.

Another high-profile example occurred was seen in Bordeaux in 2018 when Ford threatened to shut down a facility. The French government took an aggressive line and vowed in to make the US automaker pay for laid-off staff, a clean-up of the plant, and support efforts to implant new industrial activity there. The French finance minister Bruno Le Maire even made an uncharacteristic public admonishment of a foreign company for failing to return his phone calls. Given the global shifts in supply chain, economic nationalism, and reshoring, we can expect to see more of regeneration-type activity.

Closer to home, FDI has been a significant contributor to Northern Ireland's peace process and continues to offer well-educated young people the chance to find professional careers at home instead of having to emigrate, as well as attracting new and diverse communities from Poland, Brazil, and India to make Northern Ireland home and dilute the narrow green and orange tribal identities.

The late John Hume was one of the first local politicians to recognise this and did much for his native and beloved city of Derry to persuade US politicians and corporate America that their investments in the region would be safe and sustainable in spite of the backdrop of the ongoing troubles. Notable early successes include Seagate, DuPont, and Raytheon, followed by more recent technology arrivals such as Allstate, One Source, and Fujitsu. After the Good Friday Agreement was signed in 1998, who can forget the spectacle of the 'Chuckle Brothers" former arch-rivals Ian Paisley and Martin McGuiness going on charm offensives to woo corporate America to Northern Ireland? It was a highly effective partnership between the politicians and the local investment agency Invest Northern Ireland, and from 2000 to 2010, twenty-one thousand jobs were created across 224 projects by foreign investors in the region.

OCO played its part too and was able to use performance data from fDi Markets, aligned with a detailed skills and business audit to showcase and benchmark the strength and depth of the IT and software development cluster in the region with specialisms in trading platforms, fintech, and more recently, cyber. We developed and evidenced the claim that outside London, Belfast was the number-one region for software R&D. That kind of headline gets investor attention. This evidence base helped underwrite the efforts of the Invest NI sales teams in key markets such as London and New York to make the business case to attract new investment. Today, Belfast is host to major global fintech players such as Liberty, Fintru, Euronext, TSYS, Vela, CME Group, and First Derivatives.

Belfast has also been able to leverage its troubled past and security situation to foster a cyber-intelligence cluster given its proximity to MOD infrastructure, skills, and security clearances. OCO has forged an important trade and investment corridor between Belfast and Baltimore, Maryland, in this space, taking advantage of the complementary infrastructure, centers of excellence (CSIT in Belfast and University of Maryland in Baltimore), proximity to the NSA and DC agencies, but enjoying a much lower cost base, and the two cities have more than forty firms between them involved in reciprocal trade and investment collaborations.

In an era of populist leaders, ascendant economic nationalism, the rise and ambition of China, and the exposure of the pandemic, FDI has become even more political than at any time in my career. This means countries are enacting legislation to protect certain 'critical' industries from foreign takeover or involvement, red-listing source countries on the basis of their 'values' or political regimes, disincentivizing foreign talent with visa restrictions or arduous and expensive screening processes.

The International Monetary Fund (IMF) reported that in 2022, countries imposed almost three thousand new restrictions on international trade, up from fewer than one thousand in 2019.[10] These new rules increased use of mandatory notification requirements, expanded the number of sectors being regulated, and brought more attention on the identity of the investor. Reforms have been introduced in the United States, Canada, the United Kingdom, France, Germany, Spain, Italy, India, Australia, and Japan. In addition, an EU regulation from 2020 encouraged those EU Member States that do not currently have their own regime (just under half) to introduce one. In 2022, the number of countries submitting notifications for screening increased from thirteen to seventeen, with a total of 423 notifications.[11] While the introduction of these regulations often predates COVID-19, the pandemic did serve as a catalyst to fast-track legislation.

This will likely dampen the volume of projects/capital flows in the short- to medium-term and redefine trade and investment corridors based on political agendas rather than free market economics. The net effect will be reduced competitiveness and more market inefficiencies, at least in the short term, until pragmatism prevails. And the job of FDI attraction will become much harder and more highly regulated.

I continue to believe that successful companies and markets are hardwired to expand in countries where the returns to their shareholders are maximized. Nevertheless, the influence of politics in these decisions cannot be underestimated, and when things go wrong, as they have done recently in Ukraine, there are significant impacts on global supply chains. Leading automotive brands such as Skoda and BMW, who have significant production plants in the country, have been left highly exposed to the war, and in 2022 were unable to complete deliveries.

Foreign investment and trade with Russia from NATO countries has all but stopped, while those neighbouring countries likely to be exposed to Russian aggression are likely to see FDI projects stalled or reversed. On the other hand, the Gulf, Turkey, India, and China are opening their arms to new trade and investment routes arising from the Western sanctions on Russia, which is far from the intended effect of these sanctions. So there are winners and losers in every conflict, and not always the ones we expect.

---

[10]International Monetary Fund, World Economic Outlook published, October 2023 (https://www.imf.org/en/Publications/WEO/Issues/2023/10/10/world-economic-outlook-october-2023).

[11]European Commission, Third annual report on the screening of foreign direct investments into the Union, 2023 (https://ec.europa.eu/transparency/documents-register/detail?ref=COM(2023)590&lang=en).

CHAPTER 4

The Business of FDI

One of the most common claims by government-backed, investment-promotion agencies is that they run at the speed of business; in other words, they are agile, responsive, commercial, and user-friendly. To deliver this promise, they need to organise and operate like a business and potentially incentivise staff to reward outcomes. This is not always possible in a highly regulated and restrictive public-sector environment.

I recall some colleagues from JETRO, the Japan investment agency, being late for an important investor meeting with an automotive components manufacturer in rural Oxfordshire. Punctuality is not normally an issue for the nation that invented Just in Time manufacturing. However, in this instance the agency expenses policy restricted travel exclusively to public transport, and the executives were forced to take a train, and then an irregularly scheduled local bus, and lastly walk the last three miles up country lanes on a 28C day in August.

A favorite quote from my career in FDI comes from Manny Mencia, the former president of International Trade and Investment at Enterprise Florida, who is one of the most celebrated and respected economic development professionals in the United States and one I am proud to describe as a dear friend. On one occasion, when we were dealing with a tricky investor issue needing regulatory intervention from the state, and I suggested we would have to revert to the company with challenging news, Manny was quick to point out to me that we (Enterprise Florida) are in the yes business, not the no business, so find the workaround!

It's important to start this chapter by unpacking what we mean by the FDI 'business', as it varies according to a country's stage of development. For nations in the early stages of their economic development, FDI policy really is a function of government as it interfaces with foreign-owned businesses seeking to establish in their territory, while for more mature nations, regions, and cities it becomes much more a competitive business transaction, and the skills and processes needed to secure the deal are much more akin to a professional services firm than a government department, hence the popularity of the agency model.

Table 4.1: Stages of the FDI 'Business'

Stage of IPA	Image building	Facilitation	Attraction	Asset building
Activities	Improving business environment	Capturing and licensing foreign investors	Proactive Marketing of the FDI opportunities	Strategic targeting of high value FDI with specific propositions
Target	Basic industries, agri-food, minerals, mining	Manufacturing and services – eg BPO	Higher value manufacturing	HQs, R&D, VC backed Start ups
Motive	Resource seeking	Market seeking	Efficiency seeking Lower costs Technology and skills	Asset seeking Regulations (tax), brands, tech
Proposition/ Investor Offer	Land and licensing	Buildings and SEZs, capital grants	Training and wage subsidy	Skills and tech
Examples	Low Income Countries	Low to Middle Income Countries	Middle to Upper Income Countries	High Income Countries

Stage 1: Image Building

For emerging countries, accepting and licensing foreign companies to operate in their jurisdiction is regarded as a progressive and liberal intervention and often heavily resisted by national monopolies or dominant local players who prefer the status quo and a protected/closed competitive environment. In these countries, the role of government is to improve the business environment and level the playing field and regulatory environment for foreign companies. The international measure of FDI attractiveness was always the Ease of Doing Business report compiled each year by the World Bank. This was discontinued in 2021 after 'data irregularities', but another similar index of business climate is being developed by the bank.

Figure 4.1: An Example of the Ease of Doing Business index

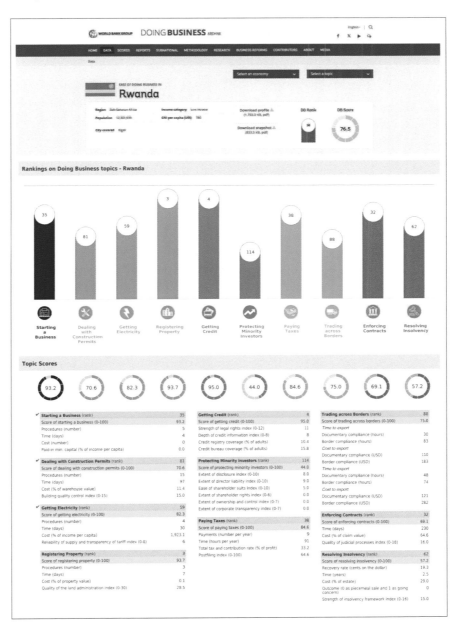

The World Bank also provides consulting and capacity building services to countries that are trying to improve their regulatory and business environment to attract foreign firms. This stage is called image building.

Many African nations and Southeast Asia economies are at this regulatory stage of their FDI journey, and it makes it difficult for them to attract highly regulated, multinational companies that cannot sanction the political and economic risk involved. By contrast, investors and entrepreneurs from fast-growing emerging markets such as India and China are much more at ease in such environments and actually thrive in the regulatory grey space where environmental rules, labor rights, and planning are opaque or pliable. Since 2010, India and China have accounted for 9 per cent of all FDI projects into Africa, compared to 5 per cent of all projects to the rest of the world. China in particular is in the ascendency, with growth of 42 per cent (CAGR) since 2010 compared to 30 per cent from the United States and 26 per cent from the United Kingdom.

Stage 2: Facilitation

At the next stage of development, when the regulatory and business environment is clear, developing countries will establish government departments or agencies to facilitate investment. That involves creating a vetting and approval center for the foreign company to obtain an investment licence. And there is much competition among such nations to demonstrate ease and effectiveness of their FDI approval systems. OCO undertook several investment policy reviews in emerging markets for UNCTAD, World Bank, and UNDP, and I recall meeting 'investors' in seedy hotel bars in West Africa from China, the Middle East, and India, who looked like frontiersmen sent by their firms to find a way to unlock the market, work around the red tape, and told to not come home if they fail. Typical investments were resource-driven and involved exploitation or primary processing of basic commodities in agri-food, fishing, and minerals, sadly with minimal impact on the productivity of the local economy.

In 2005 I recall with sadness one such example in Benin, when I was working on an engagement for UNCTAD doing an investment policy review. One of the few products from this country that attracts a premium in export markets is the locally caught shrimp. A number of foreign firms have established factories to add value to the catch, which involves employing nimble-fingered young women (who should be in full-time education) to sort and peel them for freezing, packing, and shipping to Europe and Asia, where in spite of tariffs, the value of a kilo of shrimp constitutes the monthly salary of one of the workers.

From 2014–16, OCO was engaged on an EU aid-funded program to train and build capacity at BKPM, the Indonesian investment agency. Our work involved training what was essentially a compliance and permitting bureaucracy in the art of client service and investment promotion. At the outset of the engagement, the CEO proudly toured me around an extensive investor-permitting center, which looked like the visa section of an embassy, where anxious investors and their delegates waited patiently to get to a window where they had their documents scrutinized and reviewed prior to having their trading licence revoked, renewed (annually), or approved for the first time. The gayly colored batik shirts of the civil servants betrayed the fact that they saw themselves as a regulatory gate and a source of revenue for the Indonesian government (such as the tax collecting department), and their concept of customer service was anathema to welcoming foreign investment. The presence of large numbers of state monopolies or national industries in such countries often linked to political dynasties means that each foreign-investment proposal is scrutinized for the threat it might pose to such arrangements.

More recently (2016–present), OCO has been working in Saudi Arabia, whereas part of the Vision 2030 of the Crown Prince Mohamed bin Salman, the country is opening up to foreign investment outside the petrochemical sector to help diversify the economy and bring employment opportunities to educated young Saudis.

When we began the assignment, we noted that the largest department of the Saudi Arabian Government Investment Agency (SAGIA) was the investor licensing department who approve the applications of foreign companies to establish in the kingdom. The investment promotion, policy, and sector teams combined were significantly smaller than this team, which explains a lot about the mindset in developing countries towards FDI, somethingto be scrutinized, investor permitting as a source of government income, and essentially a government bureaucracy not to welcome but to regulate foreign investment.

SAGIA (now called MISA) has made significant strides in evolving to become a fully functioning investment attraction agency in the last five years and has been recognized by World Bank and other leading institutions for the progress it has made on regulatory reform, the investment licensing process, and its proactive targeting and recruitment of investors in core priority sectors.

Stage 3: Investment Attraction

In more mature economies, which have been though the image building and facilitation stages of investment attraction, the next stage is to develop a proactive attraction strategy, with services to support the investor awareness and understanding of the opportunity and if successful to help land and embed the project with access to local content, supply chains and skills. The focus is largely on export-oriented manufacturing and services FDI, which are highly mobile and competitive to attract but offer strong economic development impact.

Investment promotion in this context becomes much more demanding and government agencies need to adapt to the speed of business and nurture a client centric culture among their staff in order to win contestable mobile investment of this nature. OCO developed a strategic framework to describe the stages of site selection process among investors mapped to the services that an IPA must design and deliver to remain competitive and relevant. It has been used widely in IPA training and strategy development.

Figure 4.2: OCO's Six-step Methodology is Tried and Tested and has Facilitated Major FDI with IPAs Around the World

STEP 01: INVESTMENT STRATEGY

Helping you to identify market opportunities and articulate your competitive offer to effectively pursue investment.

STEP 02: INVESTMENT PROMOTION

Aiding you to develop your brand and manage your resources to plan your outreach activities to investors.

STEP 03: INVESTMENT OUTREACH

Supporting you to generate leads for inward FDI and helping you to connect to local investors.

STEP 04: INVESTMENT FACILITATION

Assisting you in qualifying enquiries, manage transactions and close deals with one-to-one support.

STEP 05: INVESTMENT AFTERCARE

Supporting with our aftercare toolkit helps to embed investors in markets and support your growth.

STEP 06: INVESTMENT MONITORING

Analysing investor perceptions of the receiving economy and monitor FDI trends for business intelligence reports.

A common challenge for government agencies responsible for attracting FDI is to recruit and reward the right commercial talents and behaviors often in a low-risk, highly regulated and conservative environment. The classic sales disciplines of pipeline development, speculative prospection, positioning the offer against competitor regions, bringing other government departments (such as planning, tax, and regulatory) together to speak with one voice to the investor, and winning and account managing the investment for maximum economic impact are often absent or uncomfortable for the public-servant mindset. Moreover, the civil service pay and conditions designed to attract long-term employees with limited appetite for risk or raising their profile, and limited opportunity to incentivize results, can be a significant constraint to the development of an effective IPA.

When I worked at the UK's Department for International Trade for twelve months on secondment, I presented a paper to the executive committee on how we could reshape our investment attraction strategy, which went down quite well. After the meeting, one of my senior colleagues in policy was furious and felt I had gone too far in my suggestions and not cleared them with her in advance. She reminded me that she was deftly managing a thirty-year civil service career while I was there for a wet weekend.

In my experience, IPAs that have been able to overcome these challenges sit adjacent to government departments in an agency with private-sector board oversight, an ability to hire from the civil service and externally, and more flexibility around contract and remuneration. Invest Hong Kong, IDA Ireland, and EDB Bahrain are all good examples. The other approach is to establish partnerships with private-sector delivery partners who are contracted to deliver on aspects of the investor service where the government has limited capacity, reach, or skills. Aspects such as event marketing, lead generation, business intelligence, and training are all areas that lend themselves to this 'outsourced' approach, and the most effective contracts have a risk-reward element to ensure performance is maximised, or underperformance leads to sanctions.

Back in the late '90s and early noughties, in the United States, when budgets were tight, many US states were forced to reduce or close their international office footprints as they were no longer affordable or there was scrutiny on the ROI they provided. One of OCO's first significant outsourced delivery contracts was with the state of Florida, which closed all their international offices in 2002, which were costing the state close to $5 million. Instead, they redeployed less than half the money to step up a contractor network consisting of private-sector firms like OCO to represent them in key markets. Contracts were competitively tendered, and suppliers vetted closely for track record, conflict of interest, and understanding of Florida offer.

Enterprise Florida can now demonstrate to its legislature that for every dollar spent on FDI and trade promotion it gets a seventeen-fold return (according to EY audit). And unlike state employees and fixed overseas offices, if contractors fail to meet their objectives or the market opportunity shifts, they can be replaced or stood down at short notice. The Enterprise Florida representation model has now been widely copied by nearly all US states and regions to expand their international reach and performance in a highly controllable way.

Stage 4: Asset Building

When a location has firmly established itself as a successful destination for foreign investment, it is likely to become more selective and targeted in its investment attraction efforts. As an Invest in Holland executive recently commented to me, the Netherlands is full, so we have to focus on upgrading our FDI stock, not blindly following the herd. Lots of developed countries are finding that workforce, land, and energy constraints are limiting their scope to host new investment. The priority for such nations is to identify gaps in supply chains or ecosystems and to focus narrowly on the technologies and international firms that may be able to fill them. This requires a more sophisticated research-based approach, understanding industry verticals and productivity gaps, and engaging with industry specialists and influencers who can advise on how to plug them.

In the United Kingdom, after the New Labour Blair years, David Cameron's conservatives pledged to break up what they regarded as ineffective, expensive, and uncontrollable regional efforts to promote the UK regions for FDI. Upon election they withdrew funding from nine regional development authorities (RDAs) such as North West or East of England and tendered a contract to the private sector to deliver investment landing and account-management services. In consortia with PA Consulting in 2011, and latterly with EY in 2017, OCO successfully tendered for this contract and won. With more than one hundred staff, many of whom were transferred from roles in RDAs, the UK government-organization DIT (now DBT) successfully built an outsourced delivery model to replace what it regarded as a wasteful and ineffective regional model.

The benefits of the model are that it is performance-based, the contractor is committed to the same targets as the department, and they must play their role in delivery. It is also agile and able to flex and respond to shifts in demand, capacity, and new opportunities. In its latest iteration, the contract includes an OCO led knowledge lab unit to feed business and market intelligence to the investment promotion teams, a unit that produces sales collateral, and an FDI training academy that ensures investment officers have access to the latest tools and techniques to attract investment.

As the FDI landscape has evolved to include more specialist sectors, new forms of investment, startups, and acquisitions, it is inevitable that more private-sector expertise will need to work with and for government-funded IPAs to make them more agile and commercial. City-based agencies have been among the most innovative in this space, and places such as Paris, Berlin, London, and Stockholm have developed a suite of propositions with private sector partners in education, technology, real estate, advisory, VC, and scaling to attract and work with foreign companies in making their city a key development hub.

Tech City in London, Factory Berlin, Station 17 in Paris, B.Amsterdam, and Kista district in Stockholm are good examples of this form of collaboration, and it is perhaps not surprising that these were rated as the top-five cities for startups in Europe in 2020 by StartupBlink.

This chapter is titled The Business of FDI. Government and business do not typically mix so well, and there will always be tension between the commercial prerogative of firms wishing to expand profitably in international markets with minimum bureaucracy and maximum expediency, set against governments who want to capture, control, and regulate these investments to extract the best economic dividend from the opportunity.

The most effective government-controlled investment promotion teams employ specialists from industry or partner with the private sector to translate their objectives and processes to attributes that companies will understand, while on the private sector side, the largest investors have government-relations teams who help the corporate to navigate the noise of government and extract the best deals. In between a significant advisory industry, to which OCO belongs and owes its success, it strives and thrives to identify and mediate deals on either side.

CHAPTER 5

What Do High-Performing IPAs Do Well?

OCO was commissioned by the World Bank in 2012 to research and prepare an evaluation/benchmarking report on more than two hundred investment-promotion agencies from around the world to try to answer this question.

Beyond the desk research to capture all the baseline statistics on the agency size, funding, services, and performance indicators, we came up with the idea of a mystery shopping exercise. In other words, we invented a couple of project opportunities (an investment in tourism and one in the agri-food sector to cover the widest sample of recipients) and approached each IPA as an intermediary/site selection advisory firm, withholding the name of the investor but presenting the precise requirements of each project—jobs and skills, capital requirements, facilities, utility inputs, connectivity/infrastructure requirements, and anticipated revenue streams. We approached all two hundred respondents initially by email to see how promptly and well they respond to an inbound enquiry, what processes they have in place to validate/qualify the opportunity, and how well they responded to the actual needs of the project.

Hindsight is a wonderful thing! While most investment agencies took the exercise seriously and engaged with our researchers in a constructive way, some did not engage or respond at all, while others went totally over the top and paid consultants to help them make the business case for the investment. It was a textbook case in how not to win friends and influence, and both World Bank and OCO had a fair bit of explaining to do, especially to our clients when the projects turned out to be fictional. However, the exercise did provide some great perspectives on how the best agencies are structured (according to sector targets like tourism and agri-food), where they can mobilize experience and expertise to respond to the investor, allow investors to navigate to the right places by maintaining an effective website, and have good connectivity to regions and locations within the country that are potentially suitable to host the project, including access to information on cost comparisons and skills availability.

Figure 5.1: The Global Investment Promotion Best Practice report that OCO Produced with the World Bank

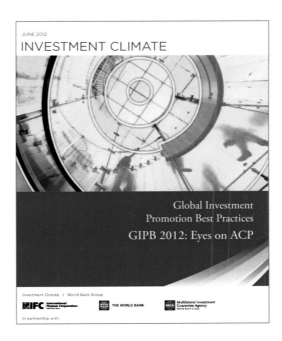

Figure 5.2: An Image from the Global Investment Promotion Best Practice Reports Shows Which IPAs Responded to Project Inquiries

Anybody there? Few IPIs are ready to answer when investors come knocking

Responded to both project inquiries

Responded to one project inquiry

Responded to neither project inquiry

Not included in GIPS

After twenty years in the business, OCO has experienced the best and worst in class of investment promotion practices, and thanks to the number of new FDI agencies and the high turnover of staff, we have developed a training program called FDI Academy. The design of the course modules tell an important story about the functions of a high-performing investment agency.

Figure 5.3: OCO's FDI Academy Modules

Inroduction to FDI	IPA Corporate Functions	The Investor Journey	Practitioner Skills
Module 1 is aimed at all audiences and provides an introduction to FDI	Module 2-4 are aimed at corporate decision makers in IPAs	Module 5-8 are designed to build the capacity of FDI practitioners	Module 9-10 are all types of individuals to build their technical and soft skills
Module 1 FDI 101	**Module 2** Investment Promotion Strategy & Implementation	**Module 5** Targeting & Lead Generation	**Module 9** Consultative Selling
	Module 3 Developing the Investor Officer	**Module 6** Enquiry Management	**Module 10** Developing Competitive Proposals
	Module 4 Performance Management	**Module 7** Project Management	
		Module 8 Aftercare & Account Management	

OCO regularly undertakes benchmarking studies to compare and contrast the performance, resourcing, services, and approach amongst leading nations investment promotion agencies. OECD and World Bank also produce comparisons, and for some governments to be on this leader board is almost as important as the FDI results.

One of OCO's earliest engagements in this area was for the revered (at the time) Invest in Sweden Agency (ISA) led by Kai Hammerich, who was a pioneer in IPA thought leadership, with a corporate executive background that was instrumental to his approach. Kai contributed significantly to global understanding of the IPA business though his sponsorship of the World Association of Investment Promotion Agencies (WAIPA), a UN-supported entity. In 2005 he was negotiating with the Swedish Ministry to increase the funding of ISA and allow him to expand his headcount and overseas presence. He commissioned OCO to benchmark ISA among its peer agencies in respect of funding, services and results/economic impact. The results and ISA's pioneering scoring system to attribute higher values to certain types of strategic investment allowed Kai to prove to his stakeholders that ISA was indeed punching above its weight in performance, while its competitors were stealing a march in emerging markets like China and Latin America. Thanks to our study, ISA were able to double their budget and footprint for the next five years.

Since this time, other IPAs have recognized the power of benchmarking to inform best practices, gather peer intelligence, and use these insights to lobby for additional resources and reach. OCO has undertaken benchmarking studies for UKTI (predecessor to DIT and DBT), Netherlands Foreign Investment Agency, ICE Italy, and Invest in France, all with similar aims to shine a light on competition and best practices. We have also undertaken broader global benchmarking of 200 IPAs on behalf of the World Bank, most recently in 2012, but these publications can get very political and in fairness comparisons between emerging and developed economy IPAs are not always so helpful or comparable.

Figure 5.4: Outputs from OCO's Benchmarking Study

COVERING A BROAD SAMPLE OF BEST PRACTICE IPAs

The following 15 agencies were selected, all of which show significant good practice behaviours.
All but the IPAs of Luxembourg, Ireland and Singapore were interviewed directly in developing this publication.

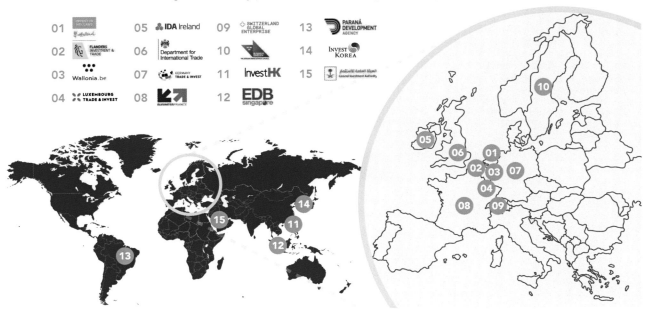

HIGHLIGHTING SPECIFIC SERVICES

- Supporting financial investments (e.g. VCs)
- Supporting talent and expats – *Welcome to France*
- New internal CRM

- Great: Digital platform to connect UK businesses with international buyers and investors.

- Start-up support through 12 hubs in Germany, to grow international markets.
- Very fluid approach to LG, with focus changing with markets e.g. big push for renewables this year.

- IKMP – Invest Korea Market Place actively matches SMEs with overseas investors.
- Outbound support only recently became part of their remit.
- Restructured into sectors instead of regions.

- Support for outward investment.
- Leveraging intermediaries: MOUs in place with Japanese companies to organise events in Tokyo.
- Use of WhatsApp has led to 25 leads and 2-3 projects in 6 months

- Start-up and fintech specialised support, with current upgrades being made to aftercare.
- Innovation in LG, new technologies being used, including social media.

- More emphasis on working with partners through *Vlaanderen versnelt* program.
- Custom screening tool for aftercare and retention. Predictive models for LG.

- Sector specialists to provide better support to potential investors.

Figure 4.3: Benchmarking Conducted by OCO Global in 2021 to Compare Best Practice Across Global IPA

GOVERNANCE
Consistently high performing IPAs (IDA Ireland, EDB Singapore, Austrian Business Agency) sit outside Government departments as State Agencies. This Structure affords them more autonomy, agility an commercial credibility, while stability and continuity of teams (and brand) is assured.

REGIONAL HANDSHAKE
In larger countries like UK, France and Germany the national agency takes the lead on project origination and has a clear contract with its regional partners to support project management and account management which amplifies their reach and productivity.

TALENT AND HR SOLUTIONS
Availability of skills and talent pool underpinned by progressive labor and immigration regulation are central to success in attracting knowledge economy projects; IPAs in Netherlands, Sweden and Ireland are becoming more proactive in talent attraction and offering support to investors around mapping and recruitment.

SINGLE MANDATE
Evidence suggests that investment attraction is more effective when it is the single focus of the organization. Efforts by governments to merge trade and investment (Sweden, France, Wales) have led to a dip in FDI performance, at least in the short term.

MARKETING
UK is the envy of other nations with its Great country brand but much more targeted sector, country and activity based messaging is needed to engage investors. Few IPAs are taking full advantage of the precision and VFM that social media and digital tools offer as a sales channel.

BUSINESS DEVELOPMENT
The most effective IPAs operate like high performing sales organizations: business intelligence informs the targeting and prospection process, they understand and monitor pipeline to conversion ratios, and activity is underpinned by disciplined use of CRM. They also cultivate and leverage a tight circle of referral partners - banks, professional services, industry associations.

SMALL BUT PERFECTLY FORMED
The most productive IPAs (ratio of project wins to headcount) typically have circa 250 staff split between HQ and overseas and focus on a narrower range of markets and sectors which they dominate; Netherlands, Austria and Finland are good examples. The top 10 FDI markets still account for 80% of volumes.

START UPS
This activity sits better at city level agencies than at national IPA, and the support intensity, high failure rate and return on investment make it high risk as France and Portugal have found out.

MEASURES
There is still widespread monitoring of 'projects' which is a crude currency of IPA performance. The most progressive IPAs also measure market share by sector/activity, jobs and capital investment, and GVA measures like average salary.

As a general rule, the highest-performing investment-promotion agencies are structured and operated along the same lines as a high-performing sales organization.

This means they:	
1	Have researched and understand the market/sector on which they are focused;
2	Understand the needs of their target audience/buyer;
3	Know who they are likely to be competing with for the business;
4	Have a 'differentiated' suite of products/propositions that will resonate with the clients;
5	Are focused on marketing though the right channels/media to reach the decision makers;
6	Are skilled in the art of sales, pitching, and negotiation;
7	Are disciplined in the use of CRM and can manage a pipeline;
8	Can mobilize the right team to project manage and convert the opportunity;
9	If successful, can embed and expand the investment for additional upsell; and
10	Hire, motivate, and incentivize the right commercial behaviors across the team.

In my experience, the majority of IPAs are pretty good at the front end of the process up to step 5, but the wheels can come off when they get in the room with the investor and fumble the opportunity to articulate their solution, demonstrate the commercial impact on the client, and do not show the right level of commitment to the sale and follow up. As my old boss Stephen Kingon at PwC used to say, "if the agency guys don't have a chequebook somewhere in their coat pocket, no business would bother meeting them". It is partly mindset: a bad decision in government has limited consequences for the individual or the team, while in business, failure costs money and ends careers.

Between 2015-2018, OCO did a significant amount of work for JETRO, the Japanese trade and investment agency.. Since its inception, JETRO was historically focused on helping Japanese firms to trade internationally rather than foreign investment promotion, so this activity was a departure for the organization. It was central to the vision of former PM

Abe Shinzo's 'Abenomics', even if, culturally in some Japanese minds the acceptance of foreign investors speaks to a failure of national industry and innovation and represents a loss of face.

As we know, Japan is a deeply conservative, traditional, and proud nation, but a stagnant economy over the last two decades meant GDP was only 4 per cent larger in 2020 than the turn of the century, compared to US GDP that has more than doubled in the same period.[12] Add an aging population, a concentration of economic activity in a small number of large multinationals, and a lack of entrepreneurialism meant that the political leadership were persuaded that foreign investment could have an important role in revitalizing the economy and shaking up Japan's corporate culture.

Not all parts of the JETRO organization were fully committed to the pursuit of FDI, or at least lacked the experience and skills needed to be successful, so consultants such as Accenture and OCO were drafted to help. Accenture helped JETRO define their offer

---

[12] World Bank national accounts data (https://data.worldbank.org/indicator/NY.GDP.MKTP.CD).

in the target sectors while OCO were engaged to help develop and qualify a target list of international prospects and open the door for JETRO executives to come in and pitch their offer.

OCO mobilized teams in the United States, Europe, and Asia to identify firms with a presence in Asia but not in Japan, in the target sectors and with the scale and ambition to invest in the country. As the third largest and richest economy in the world, but one that can be hard to navigate for foreign companies, we were surprised and encouraged by the level of positive engagement we got from the market and set about making appointments for our JETRO colleagues with the most promising targets.

That's when the wheels came off. A good first investor meeting typically starts with some freeform small talk about the journey to the meeting, the weather, the investor premises if they are remarkable (the first five minutes from reception to collection to elevator) and then moves into some more tangible points about the economy, business outlook, and the events of the day or how long the person has been in the role (next five minutes in an elevator and along the corridor to the meeting room while waiting for others to join). Once settled in the meeting room and refreshments have been served, typically the IPA agency lead person will make the formal introductions, set out the agenda, remind those present on the background to the meeting, confirm to the company that the assumptions are correct (ten to twelve minutes), and then likely invite the company to outline their investment project plans and key decision-making criteria, timeframes etc. (fifteen to twenty minutes). Then it usually comes back to the agency to respond with an outline proposition on how their location can address the project requirements and should be on the shortlist, provide examples of peer investors who have already established (ten minutes) , and in the final phase, confront any concerns or capture any follow-up clarifications that will be addressed in the meeting follow up, including any intelligence on what other locations the company might be considering (ten minutes). Important at this closing point is to establish who else will be involved in the decision and how to influence along with closing remarks and agreement on next steps.

That's not how JETRO rolls. Meetings are very hierarchical in Japan, and nothing is spontaneous. JETRO colleagues typically showed up in groups between three and five people for every meeting, along with the OCO representative, and usually only one spoke and the others were not always even introduced. There is no icebreaking or chitchat, just a formal silent procession to the meeting room and a studied and deliberate removal of overcoats, seating in order of hierarchy with the most senior people on either side of the table, and minions fanning out either side. Business cards were offered in the traditional Japanese way: both arms outstretched, head bowed, and with the card presented in the right direction of the audience. The agenda is controlled by JETRO, and they come to present their offer rather than listen or take a brief. And the presentation of the offer is standard, usually dense PowerPoint slides or catalogue and mute to the client situation or concerns of the audience. Client questions are almost invariably dodged and will be referred back to HQ in Japan, and scrupulous notes are taken on every minute of the meeting.

As a result of this rigid approach, no rapport with the company is established, opportunities to listen and get a tighter brief are missed, and unless the client wants the set menu (typically property, R&D incentives, and weirdly, a free plane ticket to come visit Japan), the follow-up and process is far more arduous than it needs to be.

In JETRO's defense, it is practically impossible for a foreign-owned entity to register and set up in Japan without their help, so they do have a captive market. And between us, we built a strong pipeline and secured some twenty projects over the period of our engagement. But for a lesson in how not to run an investor meeting, I cannot think of a better one!

The best-performing IPAs tend to do less better. By that I mean they focus on fewer sectors and markets but build depth and strength in the areas where they can compete most effectively. Over time they get to know the target sector, where the industry clusters operate (which markets/regions), what events the key players attend, and how to influence them, the issues facing companies involved, and how to hone their offer to address these issues. Specialization is the only way to secure contestable investment. Even when you offer incentives, they need to be designed around the needs of the industry. In large, diversified economies like Germany, France, and the United Kingdom, the national IPAs confine themselves typically to six to eight sectors or activities and build up their propositions and pipelines accordingly. FDI is not a panacea for all sectors and may even stunt the development of some indigenous enterprise.

An analysis of investment trends shows that the same locations are consistently winning multiple investment projects in key sectors, and it is often the same ones. Unless you have a comparable or better offer than such places, don't even bother trying to compete

Table 5.5: Cities that Consistently Win Multiple fDi Investment Projects in Strategic Sectors (2017–23)

Life sciences R&D	Software & IT HQ	Cybersecurity
Singapore	London	London
San Diego	Singapore	Singapore
Shanghai	Dublin	Dubai
Boston	Dubai	New York

Source: Financial Times, fDi Markets database (https://www.fdimarkets.com/)

To conclude, the best performing investment promotion agencies design their processes around the needs of their clients, are focused on a small number of markets and narrowly defined sectors, they adopt a disciplined and structured approach to client engagement and are in it for the long term. Too many agencies switch up teams, sectors and markets in response to government policy whims which undermine the stability and continuity of relationships that investors value.

CHAPTER 6

Account Management

Account management, aftercare, aftersales, business retention, and expansion are all terms used by IPAs and EDOs to describe the relationship with the investor once they have established a presence in the new location. Most IPAs I have encountered tend to put more resources, marketing and sales effort, and priority on attracting new investment, perhaps because the new projects capture the headlines and generate more political capital.

Yet all of the evidence shows that reinvestment and expansion typically create more jobs and economic impact than new investment where there may be a reluctance to place big bets until the facility establishes itself and the business case is proven. Since 2010 new greenfield investment has created an average of 129 jobs and $50m investment while expansions have averaged 169 jobs and $54m investment. UNCTAD data also shows that 60 per cent of FDI in developed economies and 50 per cent in developing countries is reinvestment by foreign investors in their existing overseas subsidiaries.

Moreover, if we want to model an IPA on the private sector sales model, then the emphasis placed on protecting and growing existing clients at 80 per cent versus 20 per cent focus on new business is almost precisely the inverse proportions to a typical IPA. I have even come across some agencies where there are no resources applied to account management, and all the effort (and the targets and measures) is on attracting new business. The pandemic was a sharp reminder for many agencies that in the absence of new business opportunities, knowing and looking after your existing clients, helping them navigate the supply chain and travel restrictions, and avail of government rescue funding schemes are critical parts of the service.

Another challenge is that many IPA pitchbooks, websites, and services are designed around attracting new investments and supporting clients with market orientation, site selection, connecting them to skills and local supply chains, and helping them navigate funding and incentives for which they might qualify.

Once the client has established a presence in the location, they may not need these supports and will likely build their own networks and capabilities. Therefore, the services of an IPA focused on landing new business will not be relevant.

However, that misses the point. A good aftercare/account management program will develop different tools and services to help existing investors continually defend their operation to HQ, anticipate and support proposals for expansion and upgrading (when the location may be competing with other sites within the group for the same activity), and become a lobbyist for the firm to other parts of national and local government. Workforce, supply chain, and planning are all areas that a good account-management program should encapsulate. Moreover account management is dynamic; there should be churn in the list of key accounts based on their performance and ability to expand/upgrade while there should be less engagement with nonproductive, dormant accounts. It always surprises me how infrequently IPAs undertake a review and cull their key account lists and major contributors to new jobs and expansion get overlooked while pet clients with long histories, but few projects continue to enjoy the access and attention.

At the heart of this challenge is the dreaded Client Relationship Management database (CRM). Even where they have one, many IPAs lack the discipline and culture to maintain and operate an effective customer relationship management tool. Even when the CRM is regularly updated, it is rarely used to inform or initiate new strategies based on aggregation of the intelligence and instead becomes a kind of dead weight record of transactions and is regarded with the same kind of enthusiasm as the expenses claim. You have to complete it for audit purposes, but it has no operational value. In high-performing sales organisationsorganizations, the CRM is at the heart of the business, and its content and updates drive the sales meeting decisions, key account resourcing, new business efforts, track results, performance reviews, and incentives. Very few IPAs use their CRM with this kind of rigour and discipline, and as a consequencetherefore, their institutional client knowledge, especially for long- established investors, is weak and ineffective.

Unless there is effective aftercare and tracking of existing investors (closures and rationalization as well as expansions) it's impossible for an IPA to evaluate its return on investment. For example, an investor may start with a five-person sales office, then add technical support, then more corporate functions, and eventually be a regional head office with 50 staff. Or a small manufacturing assembly plant can expand over time to having a regional product mandate for both manufacturing and R&D and have extensive local supply chain and R&D linkages, with significant economic impact. Measuring only the initial jobs missed out on how that investment grows and transforms over time.

New Business Origination

Business development and prospection is not a natural fit for government agencies that employ primarily civil servants. Few will have a background in sales or commercial roles and culturally tend to be more risk-averse, introverted, and more at ease among colleagues rather than building and maintaining productive external networks as a source of new business.

Equally, it is difficult for government to attract and retain the levels of industry expertise and specialisms needed to be credible among investors, or indeed be in all the right geographies at the same time where the investors live. For these reasons, a major industry has grown around lead generation in support of economic development and investment-promotion agencies.

Not all the lead generation industry is respectable and some prey on the naiveté and perhaps desperation of IPA clients to build pipelines and demonstrate to their political masters that they are effective. I often point to the headline statistics that in an average year, there might be fifteen thousand project announcements globally, of which a quarter will probably be expansions in the same region (so not contestable), with the top one hundred companies accounting for several thousand projects. A further half will not align strategically with your region's offer, and a further half are in sectors where you don't have a proposition. So, we end up with an accessible market opportunity of less than a thousand prospective clients and a few hundred decision makers. So why do so many clients feel the need to commission lead

generation campaigns of epic proportions when they know there will be narrow fields of opportunities and so much sales effort and acquisition cost involved? Perhaps we have all been overinfluenced by the US telemarking firms and US corporate audiences who are receptive to unsolicited outreach, where indeed there are an estimated nine interstate domestic expansions for every single foreign investment. So perhaps volume campaigns work in this context, but rarely do they work for foreign investment.

The most effective agencies approach new business acquisition in a highly targeted and more productive way. It starts with an understanding of the business demand drivers specific to the sector (e.g. regulation, tax, market access, skills, and technology) and then determines how well their location measures up to these needs, and how it compares with other regions offering similar capabilities. Consequently, we begin with a deep understanding of the sector, the drivers of growth and international expansion, the competitor landscape, and how we compare/benchmark against the critical variables (costs and quality).

Figure 6.1: An Example Output from fDi Benchmark That Compares Seven Gulf States on Cost and Quality for a Healthcare R&D Centre

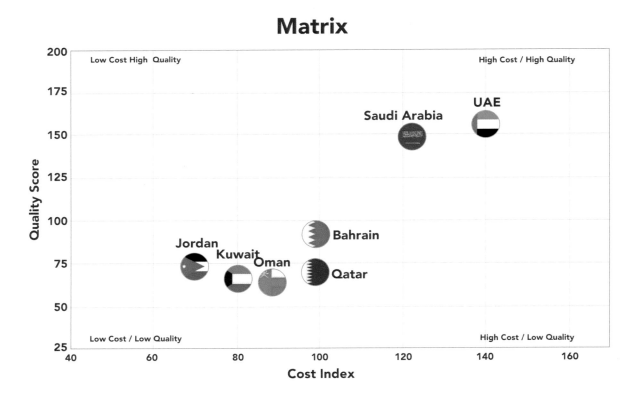

Source: Financial Times, FDI benchmark database (https://www.fdibenchmark.com/)

Next, we determine where the key clusters of this industry originates so we can get a geographic lens on our ambition and assess the need for resources on the ground. After that, we identify where the movers and shakers in the industry meet (events, seminars, associations) and what media or channels can be used to reach them; then we can start to identify, build, and qualify lists of the most active companies. Now we turn to marketing to develop propositions (pitchbooks) that will become our sales collateral to target the relevant audiences and demonstrate how we understand their business and have location solutions that will respond to their priorities. Only then will it be time to engage and go to market, and the first step will be building awareness, which can be done remotely, cost-effectively, and digitally through social media. Finally, now it is time to make some direct approaches to selected target firms—not cold calls but preemptive strikes based on solid intelligence and a good understanding of the specific company strategy. This

approach will yield 30–40 per cent conversion to active cases, compared to cold calling, which even in the best circumstances is single figures.

This approach has allowed OCO to become a leader in the field of Investment Attraction Services, and we have a very high client retention rate because of this intelligence led approach which means fewer but better calls to the right companies with an interesting offer.

I recall one painful eavesdrop on a NY-based colleague who was targeting US biosciences companies on behalf of a Spanish region that had engaged OCO to develop its pipeline in the United States. Having prepared carefully, she spent the first ten minutes breathlessly summarizing why this region was likely to be of interest to the client and provided lots of proof points and testimonial, only to see her replace the phone on its cradle abruptly.

"What happened?" I asked.

"The prospect told me to get interesting and hung up!" Effective investment targeting is sometimes about listening more and saying less.

In spite of what I describe above, where 80 per cent of the effort should be pre-client engagement in research and preparation, I have seen so many examples of poor preparedness and opportunities lost before they even had a chance to qualify.

Figure 6.2: OCO's Tried and Tested Methodology on Lead Generation

INTELLIGENCE		ENGAGEMENT		CONSULTATION	
01 MARKET RESEARCH	**02** BUSINESS INTELLIGENCE	**03** APPROACH	**04** QUALIFICATION	**05** MEETING & FOLLOW UP	**06** CONVERSION
Develop an understanding of the offer and investment opportunities in chosen target sectors. Match opportunities with FDI potential in target markets.	Identify key industry players in target market able to seize investment opportunities. Develop a list of prospects that have potential to invest.	Contact selected prospects to conduct primary research and evaluate interest in addition, use multipliers to gain intelligence on prospects.	Confirmation of prospective investors to meet with IPA official and learn more about the offer and exchange on an expansion plan.	In co-operation with our clients OCO will provide quality information and build professional relationships with potential investors.	Present business case to the company and facilitate the inward site visit to ensure the closure of sales cycle with tangible results.
• Market Assesment of Opportunities • Proposition development on key sectors and segments • Short-list of qualified target companies (prospects)		• Approach selected prospects • Quality prospects for further short-listing of candidates		• Set up face to face meeting/Call • Follow up support with information • Support through to investment	

Account management should be regarded as an integral part of the sales process in an IPA and not an afterthought. Intelligent and structured engagement with a portfolio of the most strategic investors in the location will produce more economic impact in respect of job creation, upgrading and long-term stability than expensive and lower conversion prospection efforts away from home. In a typical annual cycle, existing investors who are established and familiar with the location, will likely produce more than half the 'new project' announcements and bigger average job footprints compared to the first-time investors. An analysis of UK investment pipeline in the last decade revealed that new project opportunities from existing investors converted at a rate of 1 in 3 while conversions of new first-time investors from pipeline was 1 in 7. In conclusion, effective account management is twice as productive as new business prospection.

CHAPTER 7

The Role of Marketing in Investment Attraction

I have been looking forward to writing this chapter since this area more than any other provides the best examples of practices that capture the vanities, conceit, naivety, and false prophets that surround the FDI attraction industry.

Like the newly appointed CEO who begins his tenure by a brand and logo update to make a splash (and leave a legacy), investment promotion is hostage to the same political instincts by newly elected ministers who want to make a mark. I have experienced countless examples of recently elected US state governors, aided and abetted by the PR machine and firms that helped put them in office, go on an investment-attraction spending splurge announcing to the world (or anyone who is listening) why their state is wide open for business and how they are dealmaker in chief.

One of my favorite examples was in a hotel room in China back in 2008 when I tuned in to CNN (the only English language station I could find) to see the governor of Kentucky in front of me giving it the full 'Remington pitchman Victor Kiam'. I loved it so much I bought the company schtick and why Kentucky was the best state in the union to establish and grow your business using language (shovel ready) and technical terms (401k) that only a US domestic audience would understand. Now, had I been sitting in a hotel room in New York or Atlanta, this might have made sense, even if TV is an expensive and blunt tool to hit a narrow and precise set of decision makers in expanding companies, but if this was intended to engage Chinese firms, it was wrong on so many levels.

How many regional airports have you walked through (especially in the United States) but also in Europe

and Asia and observed the giant advertising banners imploring you to invest, relocate, and establish a business in said location? These ads are expensive and more politically motivated and vainglorious than useful for investment attraction. Why? Because the tiny number of mobile contestable projects and the key decision makers connected to them are highly unlikely to be shopping for new locations as they hurry through the regional airport, and for the millions of other commuters who pass by, this is just wallpaper, and some of it cringeworthy.

While mainstream print media is less influential anymore, and digital is rapidly taking over, I have often been surprised by IPAS taking expensive full page advertisements in influential publications such as the Economist, Wall Street Journal, and Financial Times to present their investment charter. Many of the examples are dense and totally unsuitable, while even the more effective ones like the former French agency AFI Major Investor Testimonial campaigns are a very expensive way to reach a highly exclusive target audience that could be counted on hands, not in media reach! And the problem IPAs face is that the lion's share of their marketing budget gets quickly burnt on these big campaigns with limited evidence or ROI, and there is nothing left to spend on the actual pursuit and engagement. I often joke with IPA clients that for the price of these mass media campaigns you could research and identify a dozen executives in the most interesting and well-matched prospects and fly them by private jet for a familiarization tour.

Figure 6.2: OCO's Tried and Tested Methodology on Lead Generation

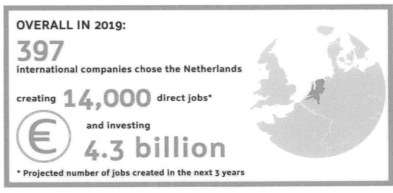

But maybe I miss the point. These campaigns are perhaps not intended to reach or influence investors but to convey to a political base of their sponsors that the administration is highly proactive and out there touting for business. Now digital media is another story and can be highly cost effective in reaching a narrowly defined audience with highly targeted messages (e.g. targeted LinkedIn campaigns), but for many IPAs, they and their political masters are still wedded to the old-school megaphone approach to investment promotion.

Another 'hustle' is the enduring media/press industry surrounding the FDI business. A cohort of publications and related event organizations have outlived many predictions of their demise such as fDi magazine, Site Selection, and Facilities Management magazine, and the business model relies on advertising by regions that present their location claims, believing the main readership of the publication are decision makers in large corporations, when in fact, the primary audience is other IPAs who are picking up awards and rankings based on how much they spent on advertising in said publication. In some respects, we have created an echo chamber for the industry, encouraging them to keep spending money on ineffective campaigns that reward them with rankings they can share with their political sponsors.

The same can be said for events designed for the industry. The grand dame of all of these must be MIPIM, an annual real estate showcase which takes place in the sun kissed atmosphere of Cannes in Spring. With capacity issues in the main Palais venue, many exhibitors will take over sections of the beach aka 'croisette' or indeed charter one of the many luxury yachts moored in the adjacent marina to impress and entertain clients. This would all be fine if it was confined to private-sector investors meeting property guys to discuss and secure opportunities, but throw in the public-sector exhibitors such as European city regions and which fund hundreds of pavilions and cost millions of dollars and you have an explosive cocktail of excess: glamour, alcohol, scandal, conflict of interest, dodgy politicians, back room deals … enough to bring down the most resilient political careers!

Figure 6.2: OCO's Tried and Tested Methodology on Lead Generation

Presidents Club scandal casts shade over 'sleazy' property industry

Sex workers banned at Mipim event in Cannes as industry tries to shed sexist and racist image

Rupert Neate *in Cannes*

Fri 16 Mar 2018 12.47 GMT

Share

Female delegates examine a scale model of London at Mipim, an international real estate exhibition in Cannes, France. Photograph: Yann Coatsaliou/AFP/Getty Images

Anger at Cannes property fair where councils rub shoulders with oligarchs

Protesters accuse local authorities at week-long MIPIM of being 'in pockets of investors' and 'selling off' Britain's cities

Oliver Wainwright *in Cannes*

Fri 14 Mar 2014 14.00 GMT

< Share

📷 People inspect a scale model of London at MIPIM, the world's biggest property fair, where more than 20 UK local authorities are taking part. Photograph: Valery Hache/AFP/Getty Images

And the financial crash of 2008 did indeed end the party for several years, and MIPIM was a shadow if itself. More recently we have seen a resurgence on interest in MIPIM thanks to the involvement of private-sector sponsors in many of the city regions touting for investment, while the whole premise of MIPIM has become more professional, and for serious investors and funds looking for an efficient way to see and compare options. Moreover, with the growing shift by regions towards attracting international capital investment to support city regeneration and infrastructure, MIPIM provides an excellent showcase for these opportunities.

Corenet, IEDC, Expo Real, AIM Dubai, and Select USA are also on the FDI circuit and attract lots of sponsorship dollars from regions, and while there is much good content and networking opportunities at these events, the balance between the small number of private-sector capital investor participants versus the economic development and intermediaries/ advisors is unbalanced and unsustainable. The pandemic has taught us all that business can go on in the absence of events, and one wonders if the inherent inefficiency and expense of these forums will ever be justified again.

The Proposition

The proposition is the pitch, or the investment offer that is used to promote and engage the prospective investor and their circle of influence. There has been significant progress in how locations promote themselves from the early days when almost every region was claiming the same things, competitive costs, skilled workforce, great connectivity, quality of life, and of course the ubiquitous map pinpoint placing their region at the axis of global trade. This approach is undifferentiated, untargeted, and mostly ineffective.

Figure 7.3: Traditional Propositions Tended to all say the Same Thing

The most effective communications speak to the target audience, demonstrate an understanding of the business issues and present a solution that resonates commercially. This is especially true in investment attraction where for the client so much is at stake. Each investment project has its own unique drivers, and the proposition must address them specifically. Therefore, the most effective FDI propositions or sales collateral need to be sector- and activity-orientated, possibly even market orientated and evidence the business case for investment. For example, if you are pitching an offer to attract financial services technology providers (fintech), then it is critical to demonstrate that your location offers access to the banking, insurance, and professional services market, has the appropriate regulatory compliance in place, has the pool of specialist skills at competitive labor costs (programming, cyber, AI), offers connectivity to third-level/R&D assets, the digital and physical infrastructure, possibly access to funding, and definitely a track record in this type of business. Understanding what other fintech hubs offer and how you are positioned against them from a cost and quality perspective is also essential.

Figure 7.4: Modern Propositions Become More Focused on the Needs of the Target Audience

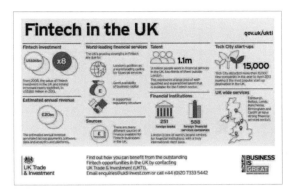

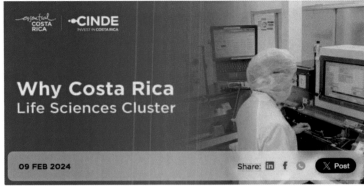

The most successful regions at attracting FDI tend to specialize in a few sectors or activities, get to know their clients and markets and build a reputation and self-reinforcing case for repeated investment.

Over the last thirty years I have seen a clear evolution of the way investment seeking regions present themselves to the market depending on the prevailing economic conditions and demand.

- In the early '90s, with high interest rates and unemployment, it was all about the geographical location, access to regional markets, and the general business environment, taxes, costs, and competitiveness, with major focus on manufacturing (Wales, Ireland, and Scotland all did well in this era).

- In the mid- to late-'90s, locations began to specialize as service centers, and we learned new acronyms, such as shared service centers (SSCs), business process outsourcing (BPO), and call centers. The focus of the pitch was on high skills and lower costs underpinned by competitive telecoms infrastructures (Belfast, Hyderabad, Manila, and Caribbean attracted many projects in this space).

- After the dotcom bubble at the turn of this century, there was consolidation and cautiousness around tech, and the focus moved to software development and platforms, so lots of locations were heavily courting the big bets like Microsoft, Oracle, and IBM. (US Midwest locations and Southern and Eastern Europe were key benefactors.)

- This gave way in the late noughties to embrace the new tech disrupters such as Google, Facebook, Amazon, and their peers, which made tech FDI grow faster than any sector in the history of FDI and offset the impact of the credit crash at the end of the decade, which upended banking and financial services investment (US West and East Coast, United Kingdom, and Netherlands achieved high inflows of investment).

- Through the last decade until the pandemic, the FDI market recovered well to pre-crash levels, and with full employment, plentiful capital, and confidence in rising GDP, regions became more selective around attracting high-impact projects in R&D, renewables, CleanTech, advanced technologies, and regional headquarters to leverage the maximum economic impact from the investment. In this time of plenty, riskier locations such as Italy, France, Portugal, and Turkey have benefitted from these flows.

- In the last couple of years through the pandemic and post-pandemic, we can sense a rising panic about jobs and economic nationalism, which will herald more interventionalist and selective FDI strategies. In this scenario we can expect to see capital flight and consolidation in safer havens, like the more established G8 economies.

Figure 7.5: Number of Manufacturing and Services FDI Projects Through the Global Economic Cycles, and the Leading Sources of Investment

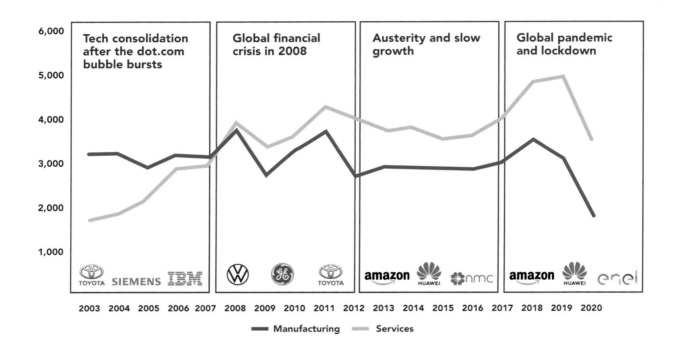

Source: Financial Times, fDi Markets database (https://www.fdimarkets.com/)

Digital Marketing

Perhaps the biggest disrupter in recent years to the way IPAs plan and execute their investment attraction campaigns has been the rise of the digital platforms and social media channels. More than ever before, this technology has allowed vendors to target highly customized content to their buyers. In an increasingly specialized investment attraction landscape this has enormous potential and is much more cost effective than the classic marketing mix of events, PR, advertising, and prospecting/lead generation.

IPA websites were for many years nondynamic and updated perhaps every four or five years, and the transaction space might have been limited to a new enquiry registration page. Today, the best IPA websites are highly interactive and offer fresh content and insights daily, have login client areas for existing investors, and are a source of news and insights for the user.

Opportunity Lynchburg is a great example of how good design is not just for the big players. Visitors are met with an embedded video on the homepage that captures the attention and shows a vibrant, diverse place to work and live. As the eye starts to wander so good design and clean space makes sure you are drawn to the most relevant content that is (most importantly!) just one click away.

Figure 7.6: Lynchburg Shows that Good Practice in Design is not Just for the Big Players

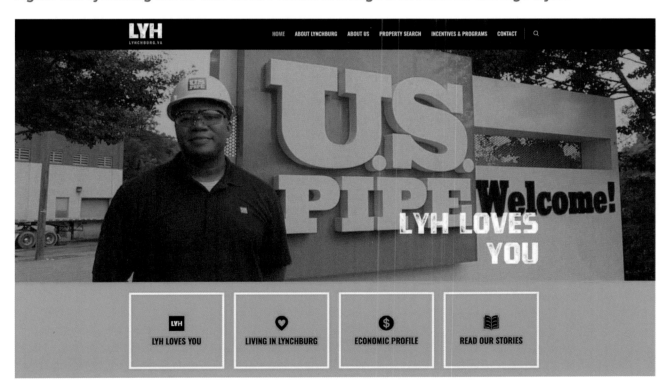

Many organizations are also turning to AI to create a better experience for potential investors. A great example is InvestChile's InvestBot, a virtual assistant who quickly gets you to the information you need. InvestChile is also another good example of a tidy, easy-to-use website, with their Investor's toolkit providing quick access to the latest webinars, e-books, and videos. More recently, they have been offering a free e-consulting service, remote and immediate specialized services for every stage of the investment project.

Figure 7.7: Interacting with InvestBot, InvestChile's Virtual Assistant

Behind the website, a whole industry of search engine optimisation (SEO) and pageview/click monitoring and surveillance ensures that the content is honed for the audience and IP addresses of the browsers are captured by source market, sector, and down to company and individual browser is for follow up.

Figure 7.8: A1 Typical SEO Dashboard Shows key Metrics of Sessions, Users, Time Spent on the Site, and all Important Location of Visitors

Image source: Airtime, 27 dashboards you can easily display on your office screen with Airtame 2 (https://airtame.com/blog/top-kpi-dashboards/)

There has also been great innovation around digital advertising in the form of keyword searches and paid-for listings to ensure the IPA website is in the top two or three results on a web search.

Platforms such as LinkedIn have transformed how executives and businesses connect and have facilitated the emergence of online communities connected by common interests and discussion forums. This allows IPAs to broadcast highly targeted messages and engage with prospects individually or collectively.

The pandemic has forced many IPAs to embrace digital tools much faster than any other stimulus to stay relevant and engaged with their clients. The recent 2021 OCO IPA Innovation Index, which surveyed more than twenty leading IPAs from around the world, demonstrated how travel and meeting restrictions had pushed IPAs to adopt digital tools, remote working practices, and process innovation at a faster pace than ever before.

The widespread use of Zoom, MS Teams, and other platforms became ubiquitous for internal and external meetings within weeks of lockdown to communicate COVID response measures to existing investors around relief schemes, supply chain disruption, and essential worker measures, while the unloved webinar became the new darling of corporate communications. Many survey respondents commented on the positive gains made around productivity, better communications, and a flattering and less hierarchical corporate structure as a result of this new way of working.

For example, Bahrain EDB thinks this new approach has challenged the linear nature of the FDI sales process, which typically ran to a four- or five-stage cycle of first meeting with overseas prospect, to qualification by HQ, introduction to relevant sector and regional partners, further exchanges ahead of site visits, and project negotiations. Now the first three or four stages can be covered in one Zoom meeting with the appropriate senior decision-makers involved from the getgo.

Virtual tours where drones and videos are used to showcase the potential investor site location have also made the fam tours much more efficient. IDA Ireland commented that an investor can now check out options as distant as Letterkenny to Waterford and Cork, involving all the right people in a morning when an actual tour would have taken two to three days. This is even more pronounced in large, far-flung locations and countries like Australia, where the adoption of virtual tours has been a real bonus.

Netherlands agency NFIA believes virtual meetings bring better discipline to agendas and follow-up meetings, and they talked up the success of their annual conference, which all took place virtually in 2020, and they could involve all their overseas offices.

It is highly unlikely that having experienced the efficiency and cost savings of the virtual world that IPAs or their clients will ever go back to the old face-to-face model completely. However, no one totally discounts the value of in-person meetings and the first-hand experience of the location ahead of important and long-term investment decisions. But the pandemic has shown the difference between need to have and nice to have.

Industry Events

In theory, marquee industry events, such as Hanover Messe, Farnborough International Airshow, Money 2020, CES, Mobile World Congress, and Arab Health, to name just a few, are perfect forums for IPAs to understand the target industry, speak to companies participating, build networks and pipelines of enquiries, and perhaps reconnect with existing clients.

Millions of dollars are spent by IPAs on booths to have a presence at these events and present their offer to the industry at large. For example, reserving a 20×20 booth space might run around $12,000, not including additional costs like travel and marketing, bringing the total to about $20,000 for the space alone. OCO has attended and supported IPA participation in dozens of such events, and the results are invariably disappointing, or at least the ROI is poor. The reasons are as follows:

- The main exhibitors are companies from the industry that use the event to launch new products, entertain their existing clients, and cultivate relationships with new prospects and potential distributors, plus keep up-to-date with the competition. Scouting for new locations is not why they attend the event.

- The people who are present on the stand or booth are sales executives of the company with the occasional visit of a president or CEO for the opening day or a hospitality event with key clients. Therefore, the people from potential investors that the IPA is likely to encounter at the show are not involved in location decisions or operations but people who are there to sell their products.

- Even in the event where senior owners and decision makers are present, their customers and prospects will be the focus of their attention rather than investment agencies touting alternative locations to set up operations.

- The visitors to the show are the customers of the exhibitors, likely to be buyers and specifiers, as well as some senior executives, and their objective in visiting is to meet their suppliers and research new ones rather than look for alternative manufacturing locations.

I cannot count the number of times I have seen well-tailored IPA executives standing around bored in huddles at these events talking to other competitor IPA executives and wondering why no one is stopping at their booth or interested in their offer. Yet they keep coming back year after year.

Of course, there are ways to mitigate this: selecting the rights shows to attend; better preshow research, planning, and engagement with the likely participant companies and their senior executives will ensure that at least meetings are prescheduled in diaries with the right people; engagement with companies that are already present in the location for account management purposes; targeting of visitor companies using registration lists; and possibly some selective sponsorship or corporate hospitality to get executives talking about the virtues of your location to their peers.

Thought leadership and innovation-led fringe events are highly effective in bringing messages to an influential audience. OCO has developed targeting and screening tools like Velociti to ensure that our IPA clients get a higher return on their investment from their participation in expensive industry events. Post-pandemic I expect IPA expenditure on marquee trade events may never be the same again.

---

[13] BlueAtlas Marketing, How Much Does it Cost to Exhibit at a Trade Show, 2024 (https://www.blueatlasmarketing.com/resources/how-much-does-it-cost-to-exhibit-at-a-trade-show/)

PR and Place Brands

It is interesting that particularly in the United States and Canada the origins of many of the investment attraction and economic advisory firms like APCO, Odell Simms, and DCI are in the public-relations business, especially corporate lobbying and political fundraising. These firms have developed strong networks and databases of corporate donors who they can then recycle for lead generation and recruitment campaigns for their elected representatives when they reach high office. It's a model that is unique to the United States where political and business interests are so closely aligned and where the opportunities for interregional domestic investment far outweigh foreign investment.

However, with the growth of populist leaders elsewhere in the world, where effective and well-honed PR machines have helped secure their political office, it is likely to take root. And we see in emerging markets the influence of PR and image-building firms in the FDI space. Saudi Arabia, UAE, and Qatar have invested heavily in global sponsorship and PR campaigns to help reposition their image as places to visit, live, and invest.

Country and place branding is part of this phenomena and an important part of the FDI toolkit today. The 'Great' campaign by the UK government initially under David Cameron (a former public relations man himself) and La France Tech under President Macron, also an ex PR/media guy with the accompanying marquee events like London Games 2012 and the pre-Davos reception in Versailles for leading global investors all underpin this marriage of political heft and PR machines. And leading corporates are easily seduced by presidents and palaces, especially if they hail from the new world.

I participated recently on a panel with Simon Anholt, one of the most important architects of the who place/nation brand concept. I was surprised to hear him say that in twenty years of tracking the movement of place perceptions via the IPSOS-Anholt Nation Brands Index annual index, very little can be done to influence the ranking and external perceptions of a place and that is reflected in the relative stability of the perceptions research. Except for one thing: the extent to which a nation does 'good' in the world either via aid, or sharing innovation, or advancing world peace and human progress. So, think Nobel prizes in the case of Norway; International Aid in the case of US aid; peacekeeping in Lebanon; or international conflict resolution Switzerland. It's a form of corporate social responsibility on a national level.

Figure 7.9: 2022 Rankings from the IPSOS-Anholt Nation Brands Index

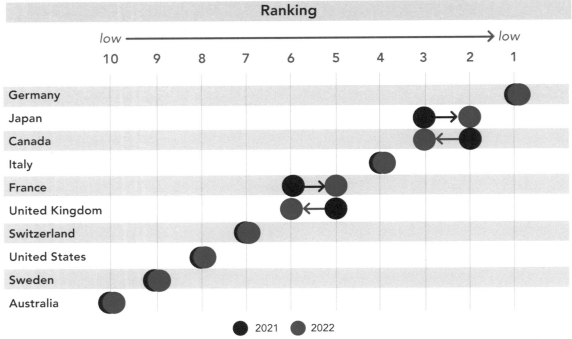

Source: The Anholt-Ipsos Nation Brands Index (https://www.ipsos.com/en/nation-brands-index-2022)

I have noted that some cities around the world such as Montreal, and of course established centers such as Geneva and Washington DC, make a point of targeting international organizations. Montreal is home to sixty-five international organizations including the International Civil Aviation Organization, the UNESCO Institute for Statistics, the Secretariat of the Convention on Biological Diversity, and the World Anti-Doping Agency. Geneva has twenty-three international organizations, such as the United Nations Office, the European Organization for Nuclear Research (CERN), the World Trade Organization (WTO), World Intellectual Property Organization (WIPO), and International Air Transport Association (IATA), while Washington is home to NGOs that employ around five hundred thousand people with nearly $300bn in assets.

Beyond these usual suspects, Bangkok is home to many of the United Nations' regional organizations, including the UN Economic and Social Commission for Asia and the Pacific and the Asia Pacific regional center of the UN Development Program. While Nairobi houses more than one hundred major international companies and organizations, including the main coordinating headquarters for the UN in Africa and the Middle East, employing roughly three thousand international staff and a large number of local staff.

It was also interesting to witness the battle to secure European agencies such as medicine and banking regulation in the Brexit exodus. Amsterdam and Frankfurt will have raised perceptions considerably by their success in landing these institutions.

If we look at the promise of place brands, it is more than a pure business and investment play. These locations are presenting a vision of a utopian future where business executives, their family and friends can integrate easily in and inclusive and welcoming society, access great education and healthcare, enjoy a rich cultural and sporting environment, and see their businesses prosper and succeed with access to skills, universities, technologies, and a secure regulatory environment. So, the pitch is to the corporates, their employees, students, and visitors and relies on the coordination of tourism, education, local government, enterprise, and investment all working together and staying on message. Easier said than done.

Figure 7.10: Images from the We Are Cork Campaign that OCO Supported

Today, a key and recent driver of investment decisions is corporate social responsibility (CSR), which embraces environmental, diversity and inclusion, and sustainable goals. Social media companies and brands that rely on 'woke generation' consumers and staff are particularly sensitive to these issues and always alive to reputational risk of placing facilities in for example conservative US southern states, where gay rights are repressed, abortion is illegal, and gender and ethnic diversity is unchecked.

More progressive US states have even launched campaigns to highlight how they stand against their more conservative peers. For several years now, Chicago has placed ads in papers such as the Dallas Morning News to take a swipe at the political battles in Texas surrounding voting, abortion, and COVID.

Figure 7.11: Chicago Ad Campaigns are Keen to Push their Progressive Politics and Differentiate Themselves from the Competition

And more progressive nations and regions like the Nordics and cities like Berlin and Barcelona make a virtue of their progress in these areas to attract next generation FDI.

Figure 7.12: Examples of CSR-related Campaigns

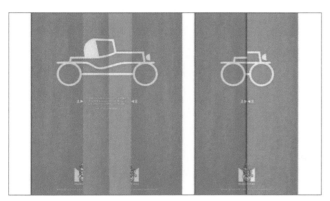

One consequence of the pandemic is that many nations are using the hiatus to pivot their economic development strategies to Green and sustainable growth with big funding bets on renewables, hydrogen and energy efficiency. This will influence the type of FDI they solicit and attract, and incentives and special tax breaks will be the new competitive playing field for such investment.

In June 2020, Germany became one of the first countries in the world to publish a national hydrogen strategy, committing €7bn to stimulate the market in hydrogen production, infrastructure, R&D, and internationalization. This funding will include Carbon Contracts for Difference that will significantly reduce the risk of changing CO2 prices for investors by guaranteeing to support the differential costs between demand and supply. In the same year, Norway succeeded in becoming the first country to

sell more electric cars than petrol, hybrid and diesel engines in 2020, thanks to a range of tax incentives and exemptions for EV car owners. These included no VAT on purchases, free parking in some municipal car parks, and 50 per cent discount on some tolls and ferry fares.

My conclusion is that 'Corporate Social Responsibility' or CSR principles are an increasingly important dimension of how regions and countries present their offer to the market. This is reflected in the growth of place brands that promise a kinder, more sustainable and inclusive form of investor experience. It is no longer enough for locations to pitch their location as the most competitive, largest cluster, most dynamic market, deepest skills pool…..Today corporates and their customers and shareholders care about sustainable and responsible investment that benefits a much wider community.

CHAPTER 8

Investor Perspectives

Government agencies' primary motive for attracting foreign investment is to create jobs, ideally better paid and more secure jobs which will create higher economic impact. One often hears economists speak about FDI policy aspirations connected to filling supply chain gaps, or technology transfer, and the spill-over effects of FDI and regional dispersion. In the end and for the politicians it always comes down to jobs, which is how most IPAs measure their performance.

The private sector comes at the overseas expansion opportunity (they rarely call it FDI), from a series of altogether different lenses and job creation is not on the list. OCO use four key drivers of foreign investment from a private sector perspective:

Each driver must be approached differently from an investment attraction perspective.

Resource Seeking Investment

Resource-seeking investments are, by definition, not mobile or contestable. In other words, the investor options are constrained by where the resource is located. For example an iron ore mining company can only invest in extraction facilities where the deposits are located, same for oil and gas, forestry, or natural resources. Albeit there may be competition among places for big energy or aggregate investment which have common resources, or within a region where there are multiple deposits/resources.

Even in the renewables sector such as offshore wind, the North Sea is unique because it is always windy and shallow and close to major consumer markets but in this sector government policy and regulation of feed in tariffs is the key driver of location decisions.

Since much of the world's natural resources are located in the developing world, the investor will be influenced by factors such as political and economic stability, ease of doing business, regulatory environment especially around foreign ownership and rights, and access to markets/connectivity. The biggest fear for the companies behind these large capital-intensive projects is often political where a regime change can lead to nationalization or seizure of foreign assets or withdrawal of operating licenses. Organizations like World Bank and United Nations have worked hard at helping such countries to establish investment policies and legislation to reassure and protect investors from such scenarios. Investors in these markets and activities tend to be large transnational companies such as Exxon, Cargill, Rio Tinto, Greencore, and Repsol.

Figure 8.1: Investments from the Top Three Companies in the Mining Sector and the Top Three in the Oil and Gas Sectors shows a Higher Concentration in the Developing World than Typical FDI Trends (2003–23)

Source: Financial Times, fDi Markets database including BHP, BP, Exxon, Glencore, Rio Tinto, and Shell (https://www.fdimarkets.com/)

Market Seeking Investment

Market-seeking investment accounts for at least half of all FDI projects because market forces dictate that firms want to grow where the demand for their products and services is buoyant and most commercially attractive.

The key motive from the investors' perspective is the size of the market opportunity, its accessibility and commercial attractiveness. Large affluent trading blocs like the European Union or the United States have an inherent advantage in that they are large, affluent, use the same currency, and have common internal rules and regulations. Consequently, they attract the largest shares of market seeking FDI with the top ten destinations accounting for more than half of all FDI projects since 2003.

Figure 8.1: Leading Countries for Market-seeking Investments are Concentrated Towards Wealthier and/or Fast-growing Markets, with Less Interest in Africa or South America

Projects

15,336

2,023

Source: Financial Times, fDi Markets database with activities include headquarters, logistics, distribution and transportation, retail, sales, marketing, and support (https://www.fdimarkets.com/)

Table 8.2 The Destination of Market Seeking Projects 2003–21

Destination Country	Projects	Market share
United States	15,336	10%
United Kingdom	12,222	8%
Germany	10,596	7%
China	8,223	6%
France	6,420	4%
Spain	6,094	4%
India	5,226	4%
UAE	4,682	3%
Australia	3,986	3%
Singapore	3,788	3%

Source: Financial Times, fDi Markets database (https://www.fdimarkets.com/)

Market-seeking investments included activities such as headquarters, logistics, distribution & transportation, retail, sales, marketing, and support.

One good example of a market-seeking investment that OCO were involved with was with Norbrook. Norbrook is a manufacturer of veterinary pharmaceuticals established by the late Lord Ballyedmond Edward (Eddie) Haughey founded in Newry, Northern Ireland, in 1969. In 2006 I facilitated a private meeting between Governor Jeb Bush and Lord Ballyedmond in Dublin on the occasion of an Enterprise Florida mission to Ireland. At the time, Norbrook had a distribution facility in Kentucky and was considering a vaccine manufacturing facility in the United States; Florida was keen to secure the project. In spite of being a fairly bombastic and self- assured character, I detected a sense of nervousness from Eddie Haughey as we entered the presidential suite in the Conrad Hotel for the meeting, even though I provided him with an extensive briefing given Jeb Bush was the brother of then serving US president George W Bush. As the two exchanged business cards, Governor Bush broke the ice by saying Eddie's business card looked more impressive than his, as it displayed the Houses of Lords livery and address with his title as Lord rather than a Norbrook CEO card. Eddie's ego was always the easiest and fastest route to his wallet!

Governor Bush made a good pitch for Florida's life sciences sector and demonstrated an impressive knowledge of vaccine manufacturing and the issues likely to be in Norbrook's location consideration set, such as workforce, labor relations, taxes, and potential sites. In response to a question about fast-tracking clinical trials and FDA approvals, he winked and suggested he knew a few useful people on Capitol Hill who could pull levers if required.

But the biggest surprise for me came when I was escorting Eddie Haughey back down the elevator to the lobby of the hotel and he asked me, "How did I do?" as he was clearly a bit starstruck by the occasion and keen to make a good impression.

He also then asked me a favor: if, after the mission was over, I could call the then head of Invest Northern Ireland, Leslie Morrison, and mention that Norbrook was considering a vaccine plant expansion in Florida. He was never a man to miss an opportunity for horse-trading to improve his leverage in securing Invest Northern Ireland funding!

It can and is often argued that market-seeking investment should not be supported or counted on by IPAs since it is coming anyway and has the potential to displace or eliminate indigenous companies. Think about the colonization of high streets and transport hubs by Starbucks, the insatiable Amazon, or German discount chains like Aldi. Yet these global brands are coveted by IPAs who will bend over backwards to attract and secure investment from them. While it is true they create lots of jobs, it is usually low-paid ones with limited benefits and often in locations where few other investors will consider. They also typically avoid or minimize corporate taxes on profits through complex tax mitigation schemes, so their value as a corporate citizen to the host nation is minimal.

Governments are getting wiser and introducing local sourcing conditions on such firms as well as tackling labor injustices and tax transparency, but it may be too little too late as independents and local indigenous chains cannot compete with these corporate giants.

Cost/Efficiency seeking Investment

Efficiency-seeking investments have typically flowed west to east and north to south to take advantage of lower salary and operating costs in the developing world. However, that picture is changing as China in particular has closed the prosperity gap, particularly in its capital cities where staff and real estate are as expensive as other global cities. Investment from the Rest of the World into Western Europe/North America now accounts for almost a quarter of all FDI activity compared to only a tenth at the start of the century. CSR and economic nationalism have also arrested the tide of outbound investment to the developing world, and human rights, labor relations, and environmental practices are much higher up the location consideration set.

Figure 8.3: The Percentage of Cross-Regional FDI flows from the Rest of the World to Western Europe/ North America has Almost Doubled since 2004

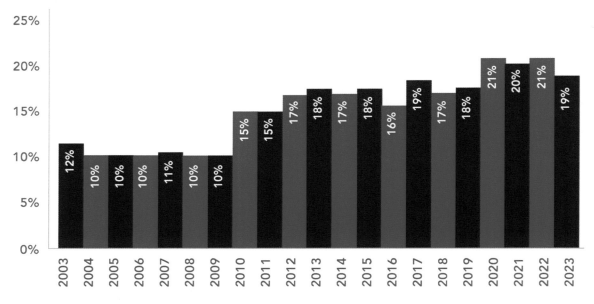

Source: Financial Times, fDi Markets database with activities include customer contact center, manufacturing, shared services center, technical support center (https://www.fdimarkets.com/)

Second-tier cities and regions in North America and Europe have also been 'discovered' as they offer cost-competitiveness and 'liveability' compared to global capitals, which have become prohibitively expensive and overheated with high staff-turnover rates. Some of the fastest-growing cities for FDI in the last five years are Athens, Reading, Espoo, Valencia, and Porto, while cities such as San Francisco, Montreal, and Houston have emerged as leaders for human capital and lifestyle factors.

And of course, the pandemic is likely to transform the FDI concentrations in cities, especially for firms where remote working is possible and for those that no longer need to accommodate large teams in expensive offices in prime locations. Businesses will still want to invest overseas to leverage competitive salaries and lower effective tax rates and high productivity, but the urban rural dynamic has shifted irreversibly.

Technology/Asset seeing Investment

Lastly, the most exciting and high-impact FDI is technology and asset-seeking investors. Many of these deals come in the form of M&A and joint ventures such as licensing deals, but they have the capacity to create high-value jobs and technological advantages. Cash-rich emerging market firms have an insatiable appetite for established brands and IP, which would take too long to build from scratch, while private equity firms are always on the lookout for IP rich firms, they can supercharge with growth capital.

The downside is that high-growth startups, especially in tech, end up in foreign ownership. Arm Holdings is one of the few UK tech firms that was listed on the FTSE exchange and has now passed into foreign ownership, with Japanese conglomerate Softbank acquiring it in 2016 for £23bn. In 2022, Arm appeared to be heading to the United States after signing a definitive agreement to be acquired by US-based Nvidia for $40bn, only for multiple regulatory bodies to raise concerns. In the end, the deal failed and the company listed on the Nasdaq.

Huawei has been a pawn in the proxy trade and intelligence war between the United States and China for the last number of years, particularly under the Trump Administration. The United Kingdom was leaned on heavily to cut its ties and dependency on the manufacturer in spite of Huawei's long history of investment in the United Kingdom in consumer, network, and security infrastructure.

Huawei has been involved in twenty-three FDI projects in the United Kingdom, investing around $2bn, alongside an annual average of £80m over the last ten years on UK-based research in general.[14] At the same time, Huawei has been banned from the United Kingdom's 5G infrastructure and faces ongoing scrutiny from the National Cyber Security Centre over its security practices.

In 2012 I visited the Huawei R&D HQ in Shenzhen with a delegation from the UK government seeking to secure Huawei participation in the new 4G network rollout. To describe the visit as stage managed would be an understatement. From the welcome LED display in the lobby on arrival with all participant names and ID numbers to the tour of the R&D facilities, and then formal meeting with the government relations management team, no stone was left un-turned and all meeting notes and agenda items were scrupulously addressed and captured. Then on to a high-end restaurant for an amazing private dining experience, followed by presentation of gifts to the visitors, the latest Huawei 4G phones—no doubt with listening devices fully operational. The civil servants had to declare theirs, but I gave mine to my eight-year-old son, who enlisted the help of the waitress in our local Chinese restaurant to get the device activated so he could get gaming!

For the Chinese, all business is government to government, and meetings with the government-relations team are the most useful and senior contacts who have ultimate say over management-investment decisions. While elsewhere in the corporate world, in the United States the government relations team has the job of gatekeeping and protecting the senior executives from the tiresome government people! To deliver effective investment attraction strategies in China, IPAs need to involve their most senior level political representations and diplomats to get the right access. Investment promotion does not really work since all outward investment decisions need political sanction.

Another surprising investor perspective came up on a 2019 trip to India when I visited the HQ of First Source, a contact-centre provider for insurance, banking, and media companies with extensive operations in the United Kingdom. Bear in mind, at the time most existing foreign investors in the United Kingdom were nervous about Brexit and the impact it might have on staff visas, mobility, divergent regulations and market access. In contrast, many of the Indian investors I met saw Brexit as an opportunity to acquire distressed assets and expand in UK market through acquisitions more cost effectively. Indian companies thrive in adversity and consider themselves to be

---

[14]Details on Huawei's investments in the UK were a based on fDi Markets data (https://www.fdimarkets.com/) and a news article: BBC, Why is Huawei still in the UK? (https://www.bbc.co.uk/news/technology-57146140)

disrupters. In summary, investor perspectives on the most attractive places to invest and the reasons for doing so is a dynamic and fast-moving target. They vary considerably by sector, market and activity, and only those locations that stay in touch with industry drivers will be able to engage with such prospects.

The current indexing of places with high environmental and social responsibility, as well as progressive diversity and inclusion policies is driven primarily by workforce and consumer considerations more than corporate strategies. The competition for talent and new post pandemic geographically dispersed and remote workers has shifted the balance of power to the workforce and corporates need to flex site and working conditions to these new sensibilities so livability and place are now top of the site selection criteria for many corporates. I recently participated in a site selection visit by an Asian EV investor in the Midwest, and as well as seeing the site, they wanted to understand the evening economy offer, the quality and diversity of schooling for their executive's children, the conference and hotel facilities for bringing teams together, and the retail and tourism assets of the location.

I hesitate to imagine how the investor's criteria will evolve over the next decade, but inevitably, regulation on things like AI, cyber risk, data sharing, participation in multilateral trade agreements, and facilities that accommodate new ways of working and collaborating (e.g. next generation co-working facilities).

CHAPTER 9

Measures and Impacts of FDI

I have had more spats with economists on the added value of FDI than I care to remember and even more on the best way to measure FDI. In fact, one of the catalysts for establishing OCO was to develop a better empirical base to record global FDI projects by source market, destination, and activity linked to actual named investors. Launched in 2003, fDi Markets which is today owned by Financial Times was the first database of its kind to capture and record global FDI projects by company. The trends and analysis of this data could offer became the basis for much of our consulting and advisory work that followed.

In spite of the wealth of academic research on FDI measures and impacts, most IPAs today still count and report project wins as the measure of their performance, and the leading advisory firms such as EY and IBM-PLI also publish annual league tables of country attractiveness based on FDI project wins. Project counting is a blunt instrument as it does not really measure the value of the project in terms of job numbers, high-value activity, or indeed capital. In the most extreme cases, a high-value R&D facility from Siemens gets the same value or unit currency attached to it as an Aldi distribution center. And there is nothing wrong with an Aldi distribution center; in fact, is may well be a prized investment in an economically disadvantaged area as it creates lots of low-skilled employment. In the same way a data center will bring a significant capital inflow to set it up but create few jobs, yet may be a vital piece of infrastructure for the tech industry.

Figure 9.1: Number of Foreign Investment Projects Announced in Europe, 2023

Rank	Country	2021		2022	Change 2021/22	No. of Jobs 2022
1	France	1,222		1,259	+3% ↑	38,102
2	UK	993		929	-6% ↓	46,779
3	Germany	841		832	-1% ↓	33,548
4	Spain	361		324	-10% ↓	39,104
5	Turkey	264		321	+22% ↑	13,677
6	Portugal	200		248	+24% ↑	21,944
7	Italy	207		243	+17% ↑	20,313
8	Poland	193		237	+23% ↑	18,483
9	Belgium	245		234	-4% ↓	8,071
10	Ireland	152		184	+21% ↑	23,371
11	Nehterlands	151		147	-3% ↓	1,334
12	Finland	124		104	-16% ↓	3,755
13	Austria	103		101	-2% ↓	2,913
14	Serbia	73		74	+1% ↑	16,018
15	Romania	37		69	+86% ↑	6,460
	Total	5,077		5,962	+1% ↑	343,634

Source: EY, European Investment Monitor 2023 (https://www.ey.com/en_us/foreign-direct-investment-surveys/ey-europe-attractiveness-survey)

THE GREAT FDI HUSTLE 65

Figure 9.2: Ranking Countries by Investment Projects 2023

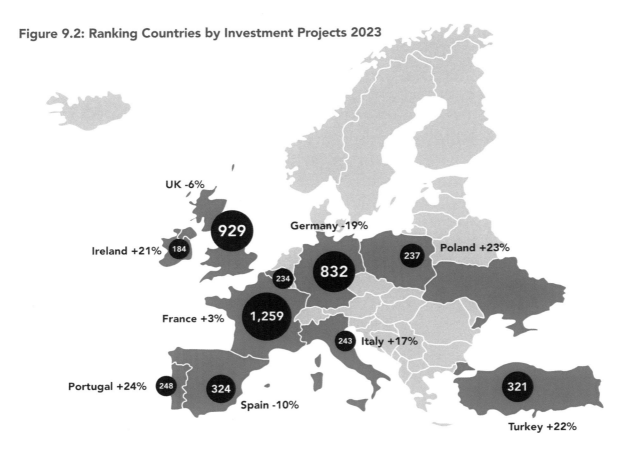

Source: EY, European Investment Monitor 2020 (https://assets.ey.com/content/dam/ey-sites/ey-com/en_gl/topics/attractiveness/ey-europe-attractiveness-survey-2020-v3.pdf)

Figure 9.3: Everyone Wants to Promote Being Top of Table

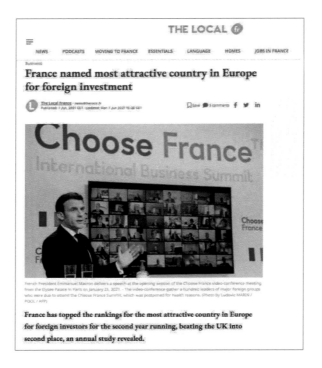

As well as projects, many IPAs do try to capture the jobs impact of FDI, but here again this can be hard to verify if the client considers it sensitive commercial information, does not want to commit to job numbers until they see how things go, or creates additional jobs over a multiyear cycle, so when to measure and avoid double counting presents a challenge.

Assuming we can get the accurate job information, another key measure and ambition of FDI is to create high-value jobs (e.g. above minimum wage or industry benchmarks). Here again salary information may be commercially sensitive, and there are significant regional variations—for example, what is a competitive salary in Toulouse may fail to attract candidates in Paris.

Activity is also an increasingly effective measure of economic impact of FDI. At the turn of the century, manufacturing accounted for nearly half of all jobs created by FDI. Today that is closer to a third, and services FDI is the dominant source of demand. The categories of activity more likely to create high-value employment include R&D, headquarters, sales and marketing, training and tech support, software development, activites that need limited capital investment, while logistics, extraction, retail, tourism, and contact centers are typically lower-value jobs but still be heavily prized in areas that do not have concentrations of highly skilled workers.

The link between third-level education and FDI attraction is well known, but the engagement by academia with the investment promotion process is not as integrated as it needs to be to secure the pipeline of skills and specialisms of the future.

Capital expenditure (Capex) and its inward and outward flow is the preferred measure of the economists as it is transparent and well accepted as a macroeconomic measure. The problem for executive agencies is that it is difficult to operationalize and is outside their control. So paradoxically, an outward flow of capital by firms from an acquisitive and confident nation should be a good thing (like United States outbound) but is often regarded by their domestic administrations as unpatriotic, while inflows of foreign capital, often though large leveraged buyouts is to be welcomed, even if there is a risk that control of these assets has now fallen into foreign hands. Of course, over time as an aggregate measure of competitiveness and confidence, Capex is a really useful tool, but for the purposes of FDI attraction, only firm level Capex, if it is disclosed, makes for an interesting measure.

Since operating expenditure (OPEX) and cash flow is a much more relevant measure for services investors who dominate the FDI landscape today, it is surprising how few IPAs track and tag this measure, and it is relatively easy to model average salaries (if jobs data is accurate), accommodation and inputs (telecoms, power, and logistics), plus is helps project the tax and social security impact of this type of investment. Much has been made of major corporates such as Starbucks and Amazon corporate tax avoidance strategies, but the personal tax income on their extensive payrolls is even more valuable to the economy and dispersion of regional employment, than say a HQ operation with skeleton staff in a major capital city throwing off a small percentage of its regional profits to the treasury.

Figure 9.4: OCO and EY Assessed the Pros and Cons of current FDI Measures

CURRENT FDI MEASURES OF EUROPEAN IPAs

CLASSIC FDI MEASURES
- No. of FDI Projects Greenfield, Expansion
- No. of FDI jobs (within 3 years after establishing)
- Capex
- M&A: No. of Projects
- Real Estate Transactions
- FDI Retention: jobs safeguarded

QUALITY MEASURES
- No. of projects by activity (HQs, Digital etc)
- No. of R&D jobs
- R&D Expenditure of established foreign businesses
- Average salary
- Tax revenue of FDI (corp/Income) incl. social security contributions
- Retail: only projects with >20 jobs/project
- Increase in export orientation through FDI
- Gold/Silver/Bronze
- FDI-Project status
- Market share by sector
- 3-5 years strategy targets for IPA
- Turnover of foreign subsidies

IMPACT FROM MEASURES
- Diversification of economy (change of Industry market shares over time)
- Changes in FDI stocks & flows (balaance sheet)
- Share of IPA 'involved' projects related to all FDI projects
- Sector penetration of FDI
- R&D Expenditure of established foreign businesses
- Contribution of FDI to certain regional territories
- FDI impact on employment
- FDI impact on GDP
- Spill over-effects

FDI ECONOMIC VALUE
- Economy value - models (different performance indicators combined)
- Changes in profits & wages of businesses and employees
- Jobs retained
- Conference hosted (Web Summit)
- Additional supply chain sales by supported SMEs
- (Example: L&P Methodology)
- Balanced Scorecard assessment
- (Foreign) Venture Capital flows in digital local ecosystem (objective: create unicorns)
- Story-telling of FDI Successes for awareness-building
- Attraction of (foreign) talent (with skills in target industries)

EUROPEAN IPAs HAVE A BROAD RANGE OF DIFFERENT FDI MEASURES. SOME AGENCIES FOCUS ON QUALITY, IMPACT AND ECONOMIC VALUE OF FDI

OUTPUT | INCOME

01 Capex	02 Projects	03 Jobs	04 GVA	05 Other
Definition $$ Value of foreign capital investment onflows	**Definition** Media/Public announcements regarding investment intentions	**Definition** No. of positions (and value) created (or safeguarded) by FDI	**Definition** Average job value ceated by FDI: Payroll & Positions	**Definition** Market share, tax receipts, OpEx
Pros Good measure of manufacturing and funds/MA flows	**Pros** Common currency, easy to create rankings and attributable to company	**Pros** Job creation is a better econoic measure than projects	**Pros** Reflects the fact that some jobs create better economic impact	**Pros** Relevant in a more specialised FDI world
Cons Ineffective measure of services investments	**Cons** No discrimination between projects Announcements do not always materialise	**Cons** Some jobs are better than others. Job creation needs to be tracked	**Cons** Difficult to capture and benchmark	**Cons** Lack of common methodology
Mitigation Estimate OpEx	**Mitigation** Business registrations	**Mitigation** Annual Business return	**Mitigation** Benchmark avg salary by sector activity and apply	**Mitigation** Evolving EY/OCO Mode

The impact of FDI can only be measured over the longer term as higher impact investment in say Big Pharma or automotive has a long planning cycle and twenty-year payback horizon. So, the idea that you can count projects and measure FDI performance in annual IPA budget cycles is at best naive and at worst misleading. The best examples of FDI impact measures are derived over time, such as the percentage of GDP or employment that is foreign owned, or the market share of a particular sector. The lobby group Global Business Alliance (previously called Organization for International Investment) in Washington DC makes clever use of its clients' FDI impact to influence policymakers on Capitol Hill by demonstrating their contributions to tax, employment, and export activity.

Figure 9.5: The Global Business Alliance show how to sell foreign investment to politicians and taxpayers

In a world of declining FDI demand, set against a background of economic nationalism, market protectionism, and geopolitical uncertainty, the crude metric of counting annual FDI project numbers will likely evolve, and more meaningful measures like market share, impact on GVA and a focus on longer term strategic projects which are highly contestable is likely to prevail.

CHAPTER 10

The Role of Incentives in FDI Attraction

Incentives have been with us as long as FDI has existed, and they have been used by governments and regions around the world with varying degrees of success. In this chapter we will explore examples of good and bad practices where governments have tried to create competitive advantage by using various types of incentives.

Incentives come in different forms but generally mean offering the investor a grant, land/real estate concessions, or tax breaks linked to the nature, value, or timing of their investment.

The most common and controversial incentives are capital grants, linked to the value of the investment and its potential to create jobs. These have been used widely by US states to compete and attract manufacturing activity and have been labelled by some politicians as corporate welfare, as they are typically funded by tax dollars from the state. US southern states, such as the Carolinas, Tennessee, Alabama, Mississippi, and Louisiana have frequently been involved in bidding wars against each other to attract high-profile investments from Airbus (Alabama), Volvo (Carolina), and VW (Tennessee) offering millions of dollars in subsidies to secure these long-term investments.

Figure 10.1: Incentives Attract the Eyes of the Press in the United States

Airbus made a $4.5 billion profit last year; does it need taxpayer funds?

Despite some objections, support for subsidies appears strong among Mobile elected leaders

Chattanooga Times Free Press

Lee proposes $50 million state incentive grant for Volkswagen electric vehicle plant

March 4, 2019

In Europe, incentives to companies are regulated by the European Commission, and one nation cannot offer unfair inducements at the expense of another. However, within the European Union, certain regions within each country that have been designated as performing economically below the average levels in the rest of the bloc can avail of European Regional Development Funds (ERDF) to grant fund projects likely to improve their competitiveness. A number of funds are also available to incentivize and commercialize R&D activity such as Horizon and Invest EU for Green and digital investments. Unlike in the United States, these supports are highly regulated and the application process is rigorous and transparent and subject to regular controls and evaluation. The United Kingdom has lost access to most of these funding streams since its departure from the European Union and has struggled to replace these programs with equivalent United Kingdom ones.

Training and R&D supports are also widely used to incentivize knowledge intensive activities, and increasingly some highly focused fiscal measures have been targeted at specific sectors, such as EV, hydrogen, and offshore wind. Film and games production is another sector that countries have devised special measures to attract investment around global royalty income when the IP is registered in the host country.

Incentives have evolved in lockstep with FDI trends. As previously discussed, FDI in the 1980s and 1990s was primarily driven by multinationals in search of lower-cost production sites sonational governments and regions would offer them land, buildings, and significant capital grants to secure these large job-creating investments. Indeed, many of the most progressive investment agencies such as Wales's WDA and Ireland's IDA became significant industrial land and business park owners, which allowed them to fast-track planning and offer turnkey solutions for large manufacturing facilities. This proved highly effective in securing FDI.

From the late 1990s though the noughties, FDI evolved, and services such as call centers, shared services, and software development became the dominant activity where the capital requirements are minimal and competition is focused on workforce, telecoms' quality/costs, and staff retention. Incentives were designed to encourage job creation and mitigate training costs, and generous schemes were conceived whereby up to 50 per cent of first-year salaries could be subsided by a grant. During my time in PwC in the late 1990s, all the Big 4 had an incentives team that supported clients to navigate the most attractive government incentives packages and were a core part of the FDI advisory practice.

The last decade (2010–2019) has been a story of rise and then fall for incentives. While yes, there were still more incentives announced globally in 2019 than in 2010, the overall trend since 2014 has been one of declining numbers.

The peak of incentives in 2014 was a particularly interesting year when a military coup in Thailand saw the number of incentive deals jump from one in 2013 to 265 the following year as the generals tried to secure economic investment.

Figure 10.2: The Rise and Fall of Available Incentives

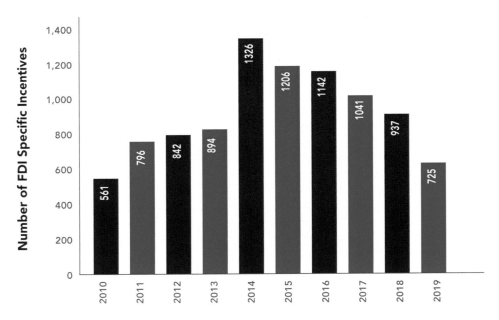

Source: FDI Intelligence, Incentive Flows (https://www.fdiintelligence.com/products-and-services/incentives-flow)

The driving force behind these statistics is the United States, which accounted for almost half the total volume of incentives from 2010–19. Next was the United Kingdom, with only 5 per cent, while even the combined total of the European Union was 21 per cent. While US incentive numbers have, like everyone else's, declined in the second half of the decade, their share of global incentives has actually risen from 43 per cent (2010–14) to 47 per cent (2015–19). So the United States still remains very committed to incentives.

Table 10.1: Top 10 Countries for Incentive Flows (2010–19)

Rank	Country	Number of incentives (2010-2019)	Percentage of all incentives	Change in share between share in first and second half of decade (percentage points)
1	USA	4,546	48%	3.9
2	UK	482	5%	-2.5
3	Czech Republic	414	4%	0.1
4	Thailand	401	4%	-3.4
5	Canada	398	4%	0.4
6	Poland	320	3%	0.6
7	Hungary	231	2%	0.8
8	Brazil	227	2%	0.1
9	Russia	195	2%	0.1
10	Turkey	181	2%	-0.1

Source: FDI Intelligence, Incentive Flows (https://www.fdiintelligence.com/products-and-services/incentives-flow)

This is in large part down to how incentives play out in different markets. In the United States, investment promotion happens in a more transparent system that looks to give investors a clear idea of what they can get—and encourages competition between states and counties to provide an even better offer. Other jurisdictions, meanwhile, are far from open in their announcement about incentives, often coming out several years after the event or in a format that very few people would understand or ever care to check.

Outside the United States, the countries where share of incentives have grown in the second half of the decade include Canada, Poland, Hungary, and the Dominican Republic. Those with a declining proportion of incentives include the United Kingdom, Mexico, and Spain.

Manufacturing has typically benefitted most from incentives with five sectors (automotive, industrial goods, basic materials, consumer goods, and food and drink) accounting for two-thirds of all incentives from 2010–20. Of these, only automotive has seen a significant reduction in its share of global incentives in the second half of the decade, but it still accounts for one in five of all incentives.

In more recent history, with the rise of the technology and digital giants like FANGS (Facebook, Amazon, Netflix, Google and Spotify), competition is centered on regulation and data protection, as well as infrastructure, especially storage and data center capacity and its attendant energy demands. Tax remains a key driver, but the BEPS 2.0 legislation, which most of the developed world has signed up to mean that tax harmonization at effective rates of no less than 15 per cent may erode some of the historical advantage that nations like Ireland, the Netherlands, and some Baltic countries have enjoyed.

In the post-pandemic world, we are witnessing a resurgence of incentives to turbo charge recovery. The US Inflation Reduction Act introduced by President Joe Biden in 2022 is essentially a ten-year, $300bn incentives program to encourage the United States and foreign companies to invest in alternative energy and carbon-reduction technologies.[15] It has been widely criticised by Europe for being anticompetitive and an act of trade war aggression as it is luring European manufacturers away from home. At the same time, countries in Europe have raced to introduce incentives of their own targeted at specific industries such as Germany's $500m H2 Green hydrogen fund or La France Tech, a startup fund to encourage investment, facilitate visas, and provide accommodation for foreign entrepreneurs and companies to establish in France.

Elsewhere in the world we are seeing a steep increase in the number of free zones and special economic areas where investors can take advantage of tariff-free activity, enjoy rates relief or tax breaks, and access secure port and air infrastructures. Aside from a few of the very best and long-established free zones like Jebel Ali and its peers in Dubai, where there is a real strategic geographic advantage or specialized med-tech zones in Costa Rica serving the wider region, and South Korea's advanced manufacturing cluster, where energy supply is extremely stable and high grade, the majority of free zones are essentially real estate plays that offer limited commercial advantage to the investor.

China is investing heavily in special economic zones (SEZs), which are more free-market orientated and where the tenants can enjoy advantages such as painless and low-cost company registration, access to local clusters and infrastructure networks, and lighter regulation.

In the United States, foreign trade zones are attractive for companies wanting to bring goods into the United States without paying duty that will end up being reexported or transhipped elsewhere. In 2022 there were almost three hundred FTZs in the United States.

---

[15]The exact funding committed to the Inflation Reduction Act are difficult to calculate as many of the largest programs are uncapped tax incentives. It is possible to see what has been spent to date at a special website created by the White House (https://www.whitehouse.gov/invest/).

The United Kingdom is also committed to a new 'freeport' policy Now outside of the EU, the UK has designated eight regions to host freeports where investors can benefit from stamp duty relief, business rates relief, enhanced capital allowances, employer contribution reliefs, and deferrals or exemptions from import duties. Of course, much of this was not needed when the country was part of the EU, and ironically upon negotiating of the Windsor Framework in 2023, which gives Northern Ireland the right to trade tariff free with EU and United Kingdom, Prime Minister Sunak described it as the world's most exciting economic zone. The United Kingdom had all these same rights before it left the Single market.

So in one form or another via incentives, taxpayer money continues to be used around the world to improve the attractiveness of places to invest. How much ROI is assured from this spending is rarely put up to scrutiny as the politicians in charge at the time are usually long-gone from office by the time or if indeed any evaluation is completed. For example, during Donald Trump's presidential campaign in 2016, as part of his Make America Great Again pledge, then Governor Mike Pence of Indiana committed $7m in tax breaks to Carrier, an Indianapolis manufacturer employing eleven hundred people that was considering relocating or outsourcing some jobs to Mexico. He was rewarded with the office of Vice President. Trump publicly claimed credit for investments that have failed to live up to advance billing such as Foxconn's $10bn plan to create thirteen thousand jobs in Wisconsin. By 2020, state officials denied the company special tax credits, saying it had abandoned its original commitment and employed fewer than 520 and invested only $300m.

Figure 10.3: When Incentives Come Under Scrutiny

The Washington Post
Democracy Dies in Darkness

Business   Economy   Economic Policy   Personal Finance   Work   Technology   Business of Climate

Trump's Carrier deal fades as economic reality intervenes

Jobs that were saved are dwarfed by others that left

I feel especially well qualified to comment on the value of incentives as one of the most high-profile cases played out in my hometown of Belfast when I was a teenager. In 1978 the iconic DeLorean Motor Company, famous for its gull wings, innovative aluminium body, and starring role in the box office hit movie Back to the Future, chose, against all odds, Belfast as the location for its assembly plant. The story of DeLorean encapsulates all the themes of romance, politics, big business, corruption, and weak government oversight that I have touched on throughout this book.

Imagine the scenario: late '70s, a Californian auto industry veteran with film star looks, funding from Hollywood A listers, a vision to build the world's most futuristic sports car, a UK government led by the 'Iron Lady' Margaret Thatcher struggling to contain industrial action and strikes from Unions in the late '70s, not to mention the Northern Ireland context of sectarian strife, an active IRA campaign, political instability, and the British army on the streets with the highest levels of unemployment and economic malaise. So desperate was the situation to try to shore up confidence in the region, and the United Kingdom generally, that the UK government was willing to fund $120m of its $200m startup costs that the British hoped would provide 2500 jobs. The plant closed four years later in 1982, the same day John DeLorean was arrested on charges of trying to set up a cocaine deal to save his collapsing company. Of the 8,333 cars produced before the plant was put into receivership, 7,401 were shipped to the United States, the sole market for the vehicle.

A subsequent enquiry by the UK House of Commons Committee in 1984 found evidence of a 'shocking misappropriation of public and private money'. Some £77m of UK taxpayers' money was lost within four years, and £17m intended to finance R&D was diverted to a Swiss bank account. None of the actors come out of the report well. The blame for this lies principally with Mr DeLorean personally, but hardly any of those who dealt with him on behalf of the British taxpayer can escape substantial blame for their failure to prevent a substantial waste of public money. This list includes the UK Department of Trade, the Northern Ireland Home Secretary, the local investment agency IDB, and a cast of local politicians and representatives.[16]

Incentives make headlines. But not always good ones. The best form are highly targeted and focused on activities or supply chain gaps that address market failure, are earned out based on delivery of the employment or investment pledges (not paid in advance) with effective oversight though independent qualified legal and accounting professionals.

[16]The 1984 report is not available online, but this was reported by the New York Times in 1984 (https://www.nytimes.com/1984/08/18/us/delorean-now-facing-detroit-legal-problems.html). If you are interested in finding out more, there is a 2004 Northern Ireland Audit Office report available at https://www.niauditoffice.gov.uk/files/niauditoffice/media-files/de_lorean_-_the_recovery_of_public_funds.pdf.

CHAPTER 11

National versus Regional FDI Strategies

One of the most collaborative, liberal, and networked countries I have ever visited is Sweden. It was summed up neatly by an Irish barman I met working in the old town in Stockholm when I asked him about living in Sweden. "Paradise", he replied. "I can leave my bicycle unlocked knowing it will be there when I come back".

The Swedes do get drunk, but instead of fighting they laugh and sing, crime is low and the women are just as likely to proposition a man as the other way around. So proper equality of gender and opportunity.

I have worked with the national agency (formerly ISA) and its successor Business Sweden on a number of consulting engagements connected to their foreign investment attraction strategies, and they are one of the best examples I can think of where there is excellent trust and collaboration between the national agency and its regional partners as well as between the capital city and its various districts. This starts at the top from a strategic planning point of view.

Every five years as part of their strategic plan, the economists and policymakers (and external consultants like OCO) determine which sectors are likely to have the greatest economic impact from an effective FDI attraction campaign looking at global trends as well as Swedish national and regional industrial priorities. While high-value life sciences projects are an obvious play and a critical sector where Sweden and especially Stockholm have a global competitive advantage (think AstraZeneca and a large startup ecosystem), equally more traditional sectors like forestry and paper are critically important to the rural economy in the north of the country, while retail and tourism have a place too. With typical Swedish collaborative and transparent spirit, the business case for each one of the priority sectors is developed with precision around what activity within the sector they will focus on (e.g. R&D, logistics, manufacturing, or training), and the likely source markets, channels, and target investors before being presented to the regions as an operational proposal for local funding and support.

Those regions that have ambition and capability (including an existing track record/base of FDI accounts) in the proposed sectors commit to a portion of the funding and deployment of staff to a national project team with a discreet budget, targets and action plan. With this approach the regional partners are sewn into the plan from the outset and have complete transparency of pipeline and skin in the game and can participate in product development, training, industry events, investor targeting, account management, and the national marketing/positioning of the sector depending on their capacity. Importantly, this avoids replication of investment promotion efforts at national and subnational levels, so more efficient use of taxpayers' money and potentially bigger bang for the buck.

Uniquely, Sweden was one of the first countries to introduce a scorecard to assess the value of its FDI successes so each sector campaign has clear targets and can be evaluated against them in the review and planning cycle. The same spirit or collaboration exists in investment promotion efforts by the nation's capital agency Stockholm Business Region, which positions itself cleverly as the capital of Scandinavia, to the irritation of Copenhagen and Helsinki, among others. Stockholm Business Region consists of around fifty-three municipalities, some of which are a hundred kilometers from Stockholm but see the advantage in participating in this agglomeration, which shares pipeline, account management responsibilities, training, and events.

Ever since FDI attraction became a national priority for nations, so too has the tension with the regions and cities within who agitate to make sure they receive their fair share of deal flow and continuously challenge the process, its transparency and quality of the national attraction effort. A bit of tension is a good thing and keeps all parties on their toes, but too much can be self-destructive, confusing, and wasteful.

The Regional Development Agency (RDA) model in the United Kingdom was initially a worthy idea to 'level up' or decentralize the economic development effort away from the national London-centric agency Invest UK, and devolve the budget and responsibility for investment attraction to eight English regions and London. The logic was that these regions know best what their communities need and what investment opportunities there are in their region, so they would work harder in their own self-interest to secure projects and go the extra mile for their community. RDAs became extremely adept at leveraging national budgets, European regional development funds (ERDF), and various sector and regional funds like Investors in People to maximize their annual budgets. This led to prolific spending on international events and marketing and corporate hospitality, and these organizations were loved on the trade-show circuit by consultants and advertisers for their deep pockets. From a national investment attraction and positioning perspective, it became counterproductive, and investors were either confused by the number of UK propositions, or better still, they played off regions against each other to maximize incentives.

The national agencies of Business France and Germany Trade and Investment do a better job of decentralizing the project management and account management roles to their various regional partners who are often better resourced and better networked with the local ecosystems. In these countries, the national agency is more of a marketing, lead generation and brand manager using the overseas consulates and diplomatic machinery to communicate the national pitch around investment opportunities and quickly handing off to regional partners when the project is qualified. That is reflected in their resourcing—Business France and GTAI have a couple hundred staff in their investment teams compared to DIT, who has more than a thousand.

The United States has an even more decentralized model. In fact, the US Department of Commerce has only recently in the last decade or so established Select USA—the national entity responsible for investment promotion via their international embassy/consul networks, and host national FDI events like the annual Select USA conference in spring, as well as country and regional roadshows. It is a pure marketing and brand-management organization, does no project management, and relies entirely on its state-level EDO partners to manage the interface with investors. Select USA also promotes best practices and facilitate training and capacity building for its regional partners. For a country that is the largest donor of FDI and one of the most significant recipients, it is surprising that the United States only established a national agency as recently as 2007.

However, at the state-level FDI (and domestic investment attraction), attraction has been a competitive blood sport for decades, and as we have seen in previous analysis a number of key states dominate the field. I would group these in two segments: the major coastal states, such as New York, Pennsylvania, Florida, New Jersey, California, Texas, and Georgia, who, thanks to their geographical location, ROW connectivity, and significant market reach, have been and will always be a magnet for foreign investors. Then we have the asset-seeking investors who are drawn to technology centers of excellence in places such as San Jose, Boston, Raleigh-Durham, and Austin, as well as the manufacturing and logistical powerhouses, such as Ohio, Missouri, Illinois, and elsewhere in the Midwest. Finally, we have the cost seeking investors who are heavily motivated by incentives, taxes and workforce training and development programs which are typically used by more economically disadvantaged states such as Mississippi, Alabama, and parts of the Carolinas to sweeten their location offer and level the playing field. Interestingly and arguably against the national interest, the most intense competition and volumes of opportunities come from interstate investment, business expansions, and relocation.

In summary, the case for the involvement of regions and cites in the FDI attraction process has never been more acute. This is because the talents which the investor is pursuing live in these places and the national investment programs may be too generic to respond to the specific project requirements which need granular input on skills, livability, connectivity, and supply chains.

The devolution trends we are seeing, emboldened by the pandemic and remote working, as well as overheating in capital cities, means that regions and cities have more money, focus, and ambition around attracting investment and enterprise to their location and are less willing to rely exclusively on the national agencies to bring them pipeline and prospects. Populism in politics and environmental pledges also influence the role of regions and cities in taking back control of their economic development strategies, and many recognize that FDI attraction is only one pillar of a successful strategy, while tourism, education and ability to grow their own communities though enterprise and progressive social policies need to work hand in hand.

CHAPTER 12

FDI Heroes

Without investors, there is no foreign investment-attraction industry. Seems obvious, but the number of meetings with investment-promotion agencies I have attended where the client rarely gets a mention is staggering. Government agencies are more in their comfort zone talking about policy levers and strategy, economic impact, and performance evaluation than talking to the investor.

I once challenged the head of the Italian agency ICE to explain why the organization spends so little time and resources on engagement with existing foreign investors. In response, they translated an Italian expression for me literally: "You don't kick a sleeping dog". In other words, the conversation you are likely to have with an existing client (especially in Italy) may be a difficult one, and best avoided.

On another occasion when I was working with the UK Department of International Trade and was invited to attend the opening of a Chinese investment manufacturing plant in the Midlands, I approached the sector head and invited her to join me on what was likely to be a positive and fun event with press and hospitality. But she asked me in all seriousness: "Would there be any value in doing that?"

For my last example, OCO organized a high-profile seminar to meet and engage with potential UK investors on behalf of the Saudi Investment Agency SAGIA during the crown prince's visit to London in 2018. My team spent weeks coordinating all the logistics of the one-to-one and plenary sessions for the Saudi delegation and the UK companies at an upmarket hotel in Central London. On the morning of the second big day of activities, I met the SAGIA head of investment to understand how things were going and if he was pleased with the caliber of investors and the meetings. He told me he had not attended any so far and was leaving that to my team, suggesting that … "you don't own a dog and bark yourself".

This demonstrates for me the gulf between a private-sector commercial mindset where the customer is king versus a government mindset where the internal client dominates the thinking and behaviors.

I want to dedicate this chapter to an examination of the firms, which over the last decade have made the biggest contribution to foreign investment, and broaden the traditional analysis of factors such as projects, jobs, and capex to consider other societal impacts such as those investors who have shown a commitment to sustainable/environmental goals, those involved in emerging markets, those who spend the most on research and development outside of HQ, and those who take most advantage of tax and incentives on offer.

In a diminished pool of FDI opportunities, at least in the short term, with increased competition for mobile projects and the emergence of more specialized and targeted offers, it is critical to understand the demand side client segmentation, and not simply focus on the companies with the most prolific investment track record, or the deepest pockets. They may not necessarily be the most attractive investors as my analysis will show.

The Best Corporate Citizens - CSR Rankings

For many investment promotion agencies, and since the pandemic and the redoubling of climate change commitments, there has been a strategy pivot to Green and sustainable investment with high corporate social responsibility credentials. Is there a correlation between the largest global investors and these characteristics?

None of the most significant global investors measured by job creation make it into the top ten Corporate Knights index, which tracks environmental, social, and economic performance of the entity. The companies with the highest CSR ratings are typically in the (alternative) energy and their supply chains (Vestas, Nordex, and SMA Solar), circular economy (Sims Ltd and Brambles), and bioscience (Chr. Hansen). This suggests that if job creation and economic impact are the priority, the most ethical and responsible investors may not be for you.

The best trade-off players that represent scale of investment opportunity and high CSR credentials are to be found in the energy and offshore wind sector, such as Vestas and Schneider.

Table 12.1: FDI Jobs Created by Global Corporate Knights Index Ranking

FDI Performance (projects 2014-2023) of Companies listed in the 2024 Corporate Knights Global 100 (those that have been able to balance environmental performance, social performance and economic performance while delivering superior returns to investors).		
Parent Company	**Global 100 Ranking**	**Jobs Created**
Sims Ltd	1	833
Brambles Ltd	2	1,808
Vestas Wind Systems A/S	3	23,845
Taiwan High Speed Rail Corp	4	NA
Nordex SE	5	2,874
Banco do Brasil SA	6	849
Schneider Electric SE	7	21,839
Chr Hansen Holding A/S	8	1,221
Stantec Inc	9	949
SMA Solar Technology AG	10	2,235

Source: Corporate Knights, Global 100 (https://www.corporateknights.com/rankings/global-100-rankings/) and Financial Times, fDi Markets database (https://www.fdimarkets.com/)

Payroll Heavy Hitters

Job creation tends to be the number-one ambition and expectation of foreign investment promotion, and many IPAs and their contractors are measured this way. At the same time not all jobs are equal and some activities rely on higher skills, better pay and conditions, and are more embedded, such as R&D, manufacturing, and software development, while jobs in distribution, sales, and fulfilment can be more transient, and the gig economy worker has been a byproduct of many of the new players in disruptive tech companies like Uber, Amazon, and Deliveroo, who prefer to avoid any commitment to training, Unions and employee benefits.

Table 12.2: Top Ten Companies by Jobs Created 2014–23

	Parent Company	Projects	Jobs Created Created	Avg Capex ($m) Created
1	Amazon.com	866	397,679	119.2
2	Hon Hai Precision Industry (Foxconn)	117	296,709	395.9
3	Volkswagen	300	132,770	222.3
4	Toyota Motor	271	111,025	181
5	Hyundai Motor	175	109,650	274.6
6	Deutsche Post	615	109,161	56.5
7	Samsung Group	156	101,046	430.2
8	LG	140	87,768	313.5
9	Robert Bosch	271	85,632	51.3
10	Mercedes-Benz Group	169	81,286	156.2

Source: Financial Times, fDi Markets database (https://www.fdimarkets.com/)

If we want to assess the FDI heroes of the last decade in terms of job creation, then collectively automotive manufacturing takes the crown with five out of the top ten companies involved in this activity and creating more than half a million jobs between them. Traditional, established source markets such as United States, Germany, Japan, and Korea are the most significant ones rather than emerging economies.

Foxconn, a major subcontractor to Apple, is number two in terms of job creation, with 118 projects creating almost three hundred thousand jobs with some of the highest levels of capex per project.

The major anomaly in the table is the top job creator, Amazon, an ecommerce and technology company that has stood up 866 FDI projects in the last decade and created nearly four hundred thousand jobs. However, if we examine the average capex of these investments at $120m, these are typically half that of the automotive sector, and it becomes clear that the Amazon jobs are in lower-skilled distribution and logistics activities that have more limited economic impact or added value to the region where they locate.

Big Spenders

If we value capex as the best measure of FDI impact, then the focus must be on the energy sector where there are fewer project numbers, but the capital investment can be eyewatering, as shown below: $300bn in just ten years from four investors.

Table 12.3: Top Ten Companies by Capex (2014–23)

	Parent Company	Projects	Jobs Created Created	Avg Capex ($m) Created
1	Intel	72	110,180	40,281
2	TotalEnergies (Total)	151	103,316	34,971
3	Amazon.com	866	103,251	397,679
4	Exxon Mobil	60	86,529	29,728
5	Shell Plc (Royal Dutch Shell)	109	79,863	22,583
6	Taiwan Semiconductor Manufacturing	15	72,228	19,354
7	Samsung Group	156	67,114	101,046
8	Volkswagen	300	66,696	132,770
9	Eni SpA	55	61,901	21,217
10	POSCO (Pohang Iron & Steel)	44	53,861	26,243

Source: Financial Times, fDi Markets database (https://www.fdimarkets.com/)

Four out of the ten major-league capital investors in last decade are from oil and gas sectors in Europe and the United States. Others include Intel (electronics and semiconductors), VW Group (automotive), Samsung (consumer electronics), and Amazon (ecommerce), which are significant capital investors based on the aggregate number of projects but typically create two to three times as many jobs for those regions where they invest compared to big oil and energy players. Arguably big oil and energy investment is not mobile in the first place and relies on natural resources, incentives, and licensing regulation so the role of investment promotion may be limited to facilitation rather than attraction.

True Transnational Companies

If we think about FDI heroes in terms of the companies with the most geographically diverse international footprints, who are spreading the benefits of their investment to the widest range of countries, then a very different list of companies, sectors, and activities is represented.

Table 12.4: Top Ten Companies by Number of Countries Invested

	Parent Company	Total	Countries Present	% of World Market Created
1	Deutsche Post	615	71	36%
2	Huawei Technologies	224	66	33%
3	Nestle	256	61	31%
4	Amazon.com	866	59	30%
5	Alphabet Inc	196	58	29%
6	AP Moller – Maersk	168	55	28%
7	General Electric (GE)	197	54	27%
8	Siemens	273	52	26%
9	Robert Bosch	271	52	26%
10	Microsoft	214	51	26%

Source: Financial Times, fDi Markets database (https://www.fdimarkets.com/

These are arguably amongst the most well-known global brands and household names as their investments are driven by market access, market share, and consumer dominance. Deutsche Post's DHL, a major beneficiary of the move to online commerce, has operations across seventy-one countries.

Major consumer brands like Nestle, GE, and Huawei can be found on advertising hoardings in all the major centers of population on earth, and it's no accident that Google, one of the world's leading media companies, follows them around. It is notable that four of the top ten most global investors are German, four are American, one is Swiss, and one is Chinese.

High-Impact GVA Investors

Since overseas R&D investment is so highly prized by competitive nations aspiring to position themselves as a 'knowledge economy' rich in skills, scientific endeavor, and offering a world-class technology ecosystem, I decided to examine the top twenty global investors in this activity over the last decade.

Table 12.5: Top twenty companies by projects linked to R&D activities (2014–23)

	Parent Company	Projects	Avg Capex ($m) Created	Jobs Created	Avg. Jobs
1	International Business Machines (IBM)	102	28.9	15,184	148
2	Huawei Technologies	93	47.4	8,916	95
3	Amazon.com	85	64.7	16,854	198
4	Accenture	83	32.7	18,410	221
5	Robert Bosch	77	48.1	26,374	342
6	Siemens	77	30.1	12,753	165
7	Microsoft	71	40.6	12,528	176
8	SGS	67	9.5	5,363	80
9	Alphabet Inc	59	59.1	14,031	237
10	Volkswagen	52	75.7	12,460	239
11	Ericsson	51	37.6	5,176	101
12	BASF	49	24.1	4,722	96
13	Continental	48	26.1	10,483	218
14	Samsung Group	44	49.1	13,145	298
15	General Electric (GE)	42	33.9	5,623	133
16	Thales Group	42	58.8	11,049	263
17	Intel	41	68.2	11,301	275
18	Eurofins Scientific	39	12.7	3,763	96
19	Tata Group	38	56.6	5,801	152
20	Bayer	35	32.5	2,464	70

Source: Financial Times, fDi Markets database (https://www.fdimarkets.com/)

Let's start with the outliners: SGS is a Swiss testing and inspection services company that has created eighty R&D centers internationally in the last decade, while Eurofins is a Luxembourg-based group in laboratory testing and certification services mostly aimed at Big Pharma and food industries. These two companies are responsible for more than one hundred overseas R&D projects creating nearly ten thousand high-value jobs in the last decade, and yet they are hardly household names. I rarely see them on any IPA pursuit lists. Who knew!

Of course, many of the others are the big and obvious (mostly US) technology players committed to innovation, such as IBM, Microsoft, Siemens, Amazon, Accenture, and Alphabet. Average job footprints are in the 150–220 range, but the value and embeddedness of these jobs is highly coveted, and linkages to universities, funding, and spillover effects are well known.

A second tier of manufacturers in telecoms, electronics, automotive, and chemicals, mostly from Europe, make up an important cohort of significant R&D investors, and here again these firms typically invest in clusters where industry expertise and specialisms exist, so they are not truly mobile. Capex and jobs by R&D investors are much lower than for other activities, but the GVA and halo of such investment can never be underestimated.

Sustainable Investors

In the last decade and accelerated by the 2015 Paris Agreement on Climate Change and the global pandemic, many investment promotion agencies have pledged to align their investment goals with sustainable, carbon-neutral investment.

Table 12.6: Top 10 Companies by Projects in Renewable Energy (2013–24)

	Parent Company	Projects	Jobs Created	Avg Capex ($m) Created
1	Vestas	35	6,977	2,123
2	TotalEnergies (Total)	23	8,798	25,070
3	Orsted (Dong Energy)	22	1,084	8,319
4	Air Liquide	21	1,462	1,647
5	Copenhagen Infrastructure Partners	21	1,655	11,139
6	Enel	21	3,624	4,698
7	BayWa	19	1,234	3,435
8	RWE	19	2,107	12,124
9	BP (British Petroleum)	18	7,179	17,783
10	Equinor (Statoil)	18	6,102	26,881
11	Ericsson	51	37.6	5,176

Source: Financial Times, fDi Markets database for sustainable investors in areas of carbon capture, CleanTech, hydrogen, wind energy, solar, and waste to energy (https://www.fdimarkets.com/)

The first striking thing about this list of companies is that all the top ten are European, dominated by Spain, France, Denmark, and Germany, who between them are leaders in renewables, offshore energy, and onshore wind. There are no US or emerging market companies on the list.

This speaks to the early adoption by European countries of climate change legislation and government incentives to diversify energy sources to renewables with guaranteed feed in tariffs and disincentives to continue with fossil fuel sources. The capex is significant (relative to other investments), so the investors need clarity and certainty about energy policies and regulations to assure the economics of the investment. However, these projects are not significant job creators and could be seen as essential infrastructure, enablers of a Green post-industrial future.

So here again we can conclude that investment in renewables and recycling is not truly mobile or contestable and heavily influenced by regulations, incentives, and national energy strategies in the host country.

Conscientious Investors

For some years there has been pressure (and funding by international organizations like US Aid, GIZ, and DFID) on global firms to invest in emerging markets to lift them out of poverty and transform them into more sustainable and resilient economies. Jeffery Sachs from World Bank and UNDP has for the last two decades been championing the case of investment in developing countries. This is a win-win for everyone as Sachs describes sustainable development as "not just a wish and a slogan; it offers the only realistic path to global growth and high employment. It is time to give it the attention—and investment—it deserves.[17]"

Emerging markets as identified by IMF (2021) account for 34 per cent of the world's nominal GDP in US dollars and 46 per cent in purchasing-power parity terms. These countries are also featured in commonly used indices for emerging markets, such as those of J.P. Morgan, Morgan Stanley Capital International, and Bloomberg.

Figure 12.1: Map of Emerging Markets

Countries include Argentina, Brazil, Chile, China, Colombia, Egypt, Hungary, India, Indonesia, Iran, Malaysia, Mexico, the Philippines, Poland, Russia, Saudi Arabia, South Africa, Thailand, Turkey, and United Arab Emirates.

---

[17] World Economic Forum, Jeffrey D. Sachs: Why we need to invest for sustainable development, 2016 (https://www.weforum.org/agenda/2016/11/jeffrey-d-sachs-why-we-need-to-invest-for-sustainable-development/)

Let's examine the evidence of how effective these strategies have been:

Table 12.7: Top Ten Companies from Emerging Markets by Projects (2014–23)

	Parent Company	Projects	Capex ($m)	Jobs Created
1	Huawei Technologies	224	13,562	35,304
2	Tata Group	172	16,799	47,243
3	NMC Group	161	4,013	21,303
4	Alibaba Group Holding	155	12,869	35,393
5	Dubai World	110	19,554	41,953
6	EMKE Group	91	10,187	34,383
7	Mahindra Group	86	2,316	12,861
8	Infosys Technologies	79	2,094	20,150
9	Mubadala Investment Company	70	72,330	16,898
10	Zhejiang Geely Holding Group (Geely Holding Group)	70	23,396	30,860

Source: Financial Times, fDi Markets database (https://www.fdimarkets.com/)

The first notable aspect of the analysis is that the most significant investors in emerging markets are—wait for it—investors from other emerging markets. The most significant donor countries are China, India, Russia, and the Gulf. Latin America features further down the list.

And the sectors cover infrastructure, energy, technology, and finance. Job creation is smaller than one might anticipate, and average capex is modest relative to the number of projects, possibly in part explained by the way these projects are financed.

This suggests that up to now the risks, uncertainty, and governance associated with projects in emerging markets can only be tolerated by investors from other emerging markets who are used to this level of risk in their domestic markets, are less answerable to shareholders in the case of state owned enterprises (China), or have a very low or no cost of capital (Gulf), and are less sensitive to human rights and democratic principles and are more entrepreneurial (India).

There are no companies from Europe or North America represented in the top one hundred investors in emerging markets in the last decade, which is quite remarkable and speaks to an inevitable shifting balance of power towards south to south and east to east investment flows.

Corporate Welfare

The profligate spending on incentives by US states is captured by the Financial Times Incentives Flows database. In the last decade since 2010, 61 per cent of some 6700 incentives packages were funded by US states, compared to 7 per cent in the United Kingdom, 4 per cent in Canada, 25 per cent in Brazil and France, and 1 per cent in Australia and Spain.

In terms of average value of incentives award, Canada is the frontrunner, with typical packages valued at $82m, Spain $47m, Australia $38m, and the United States coming in at $27m. France, the United Kingdom, and Brazil come in at $25m, $18m, and $15m, respectively. These reflect the different sector priorities in each country with heavy industry and mining, and renewables being high capital-intensive industries.

If we look at sectors, automotive has been the frontrunner in terms of the total value of incentives it has been awarded with some 17 per cent of a total pool $235bn of incentives paid out over the last decade. Mining and resources are in second place with 13 per cent, followed by renewables at 10 per cent, services 9 per cent, electronics 9 per cent, aerospace 8 per cent, and life sciences has seen a doubling of the incentives paid since the start of the pandemic to $1bn a year for last two years.

Table 12.8: Top Twenty Companies by Incentives Received

	Company	Deals	Incentives	Total Jobs	New Jobs	Safe Jobs	Avg. Jobs per $1 Incentive
1	Ford Motor Company	38	11.95	111,480	21,038	90,442	107,194
2	Boeing	26	9.39	33,477	16,971	16,506	280,491
3	Erdemoglu Holding	1	4.89	6,207	6,207	0	787,820
4	Tosyali Holding	1	4.64	0	0	0	NA
5	Sasol	2	3.49	1,723	1,270	453	2,025,537
6	Intel	15	3.44	8,347	8,347	0	412,124
7	Foxconn Technology Company	7	3.02	26,046	26,046	0	115,949
8	Nissan	12	3	14,705	10,645	4,060	204,012
9	Cameron LNG	2	2.97	178	178	0	16,685,393
10	Abengoa Solar	2	2.65	130	130	0	20,384,615
11	Metcap Energy Investments	1	2.54	1,150	1,150	0	2,208,696
12	NextEra Energy Resources	5	2.31	80	80	0	28,875,000
13	Cheniere Energy	5	2.13	689	689	0	3,091,437
14	Solar Trust of America	1	2.11	80	80	0	26,375,000
15	Amazon	136	2.03	167,682	165,746	1,936	12,106
16	AREVA	4	2	140	140	0	14,285,714
17	Fiat	5	1.94	10,450	10,450	0	185,646
18	Chrysler Group	6	1.79	25,850	3,260	22,590	69,246
19	Venture Global LNG	2	1.87	430	430	0	5,348,837
20	Cerner Corporation	10	1.72	21,200	19,200	2,000	81,132

Source: FDI Intelligence, Incentive Flows (https://www.fdiintelligence.com/products-and-services/incentives-flow). Note: Solar Trust of America declared bankruptcy before receiving announced incentive package

The biggest corporate claimants of incentives are US firms that benefit from intra-US incentives to locate in other states, but it's interesting to see companies from Turkey and South Africa on this list as they rarely feature as important FDI source markets. The sector focus is consistent with the earlier analysis, with a strong representation of energy automotive, aerospace, and electronics in the top table. A rough calculation of jobs created or saved by incentives shows some significant variations with energy, and particularly solar receiving huge incentives for little job creation. Automotive companies are more likely to receive incentives to save jobs while Amazon receives the least incentive per job created, perhaps an indicator of the value of the job created.

FDI Heroes

In this final section, I have developed a 'balanced scorecard' of the top foreign investors globally across all of the dimensions of jobs, capex, R&D, sustainability, CSR, and doing good in emerging markets, offset against the value of incentives and tax breaks they have taken from host governments.

Table 12.9: The Top Twenty FDI Heroes

Rank	Company	Country	Sector
1	Samsung Group	South Korea	Consumer Electronics
2	Volkswagen	Germany	Automotive
3	Amazon	United States	Consumer Products/Software and IT
4	Hyundai Motor	South Korea	Automotive
5	Toyota Motor	Japan	Automotive
6	Deutsche Post	Germany	Transportation and Warehousing
7	Robert Bosch	Germany	Automotive
8	Siemens	Germany	Industrial Equipment
9	LG	South Korea	Consumer Products
10	Intel	United States	Semiconductors
11	AP Moller – Maersk	Denmark	Transportation and Warehousing
12	Foxconn	Taiwan	Electronic Components
13	Microsoft	United States	Software and IT
14	Alphabet	United States	Software and IT
15	TotalEnergies (Total)	France	Energy
16	Huawei Technologies	China	Communications
17	Deloitte	United States	Business Services
18	Tata Group	India	Software and IT
19	General Electric (GE)	United States	Industrial Equipment
20	IBM	United States	Software and IT

In the age of zero carbon, it is ironic that a quarter of the top twenty most positive impact foreign investors are in the automotive sector. Of course, that reflects a decade look back on their contribution to job creation, high-value R&D, capital expenditure, and corporate social responsibility.

While many of these corporations are now at the forefront of electric vehicle innovation and planning for a post-combustion engine future, the enthusiasm of national governments to solicit and expand investment from firms in this sector seems well founded in terms of economic and societal benefits.

The number-one most influential and acceptable foreign investor in the last decade has been consumer electronics manufacturing conglomerate Samsung from South Korea. As a leading consumer brand (from mobile phones to fridges) as well as industrial giant (shipping to semiconductors), Samsung understand its impact on the countries where it invests is an important variable for its brand value and loyalty. The company accounts for 20 per cent of Korean exports.

German technology and energy giant Siemens remains in the top ten and continues to have significant influence thanks to its global footprint and our reliance on its products in all aspects of our lives. It is a major player in the 'mobility business' from trains to smart infrastructure, offshore wind and power generation, smart cities, grids, and digital innovation, and future worlds of AI and robotics. Siemens, thanks to relentless innovation, is active in all aspect of Industry 4.0 and has shown a capacity to maintain its dominant position in the sectors where it operates.

On this top twenty list, seven of the best FDI companies in the world come from the United States; four from Germany; three from South Korea; and one each from China, Denmark, France, India, Japan, and Taiwan. This is in line with the global importance of these countries as leading sources of FDI.

The growing importance of the ecommerce sector and related logistics business is reflected by the presence of Amazon and Deutsche Post (DHL) on the top twenty list. There are a couple of leading players from the world of consulting, finance and professional services—IBM, Accenture, Deloitte, and arguably Tata, but it is notable that only Google and Amazon of the FANGs (Facebook, Apple, Netflix, Google) make the top twenty.

Huawei's impact and ambition as a significant global investor in the sensitive mobile telecoms and equipment sector has been challenged by protectionism and fears about China's broader agenda heavily influenced by the United States, but there is no disputing its contribution to job creation, R&D and emerging markets footprint during the last decade.

In summary, big manufacturing, from automotive to electronics, still dominates the headlines for FDI in 2021, and the tech, social media giants, big pharma, and financial services are notable by their absence from this list.

As I review this analysis 12 months after I undertook the research, it strikes me that the FDI Heroes rankings are extremely dynamic and worth revisiting on an annual basis, possibly culminating in a recognition awards event where we honor the most impactful investors. To be continued…

CHAPTER 13

What the Future Holds

As Mark Twain once said, rumors of my death have been greatly exaggerated. Trump's policies were expected to end globalization and isolate China. They have not. Britain's departure from the EU was supposed to hasten the implosion of the European Union. It has, in fact, strengthened the power of the European trading bloc. Remote working practices imposed by the pandemic threatened to end the role of cities as engines of our economies; they have not (albeit the office/homework balance has shifted). Trade without travel has become a reality, and buyers and suppliers have embraced technology platforms to connect and transact remotely. And although foreign investment experienced a significant drop in 2020 (35 per cent compared to 2019), 2021 has seen a rapid bounce back in capital flows via IPOs, M&A, and more recently, new FDI projects in resilient sectors that are responsible for more FDI projects now than before the pandemic.

As the graph shows below, these resilient sectors fit into different groups. On the right-hand side are the large sectors such as software/IT and professional services (finance, legal, and consulting) that are key to delivering economic transition, while on the left are the smaller sectors that define this transition—semiconductors, gaming/digital content, batteries, and logistics (supporting the shift to ecommerce). And then there is renewable energy. In 2019 there were thirty-two FDI projects in this sector compared to 189 in 2022—a growth of 491 per cent.

Figure 13.1: Most Resilient Sectors for FDI Based on Number and Growth of FDI Projects (2019–22)

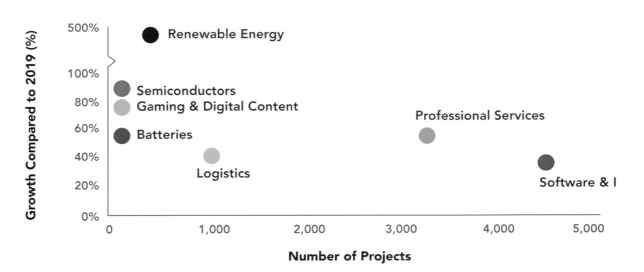

Source: Financial Times, fDi Markets database (https://www.fdimarkets.com/)

Specialization: less but better FDI

The post-pandemic landscape for FDI is likely to evolve over time to respond to new sector and technology priorities such as environmental tech, mobility, AI, precision medicine, and digitization, which will drive the project volumes and increased specialization by nations that aspire to become centers of excellence for such industries of the future. Skills and incentives (based on industrial priorities), as well as regulation will narrow the competitive field for such projects so we can anticipate lower volumes but higher value/impact investment.

Protectionism through regulation

Protectionism will be a lasting consequence of post-pandemic economic self-interest amongst nations as well as new geopolitical alliances and trade agreements, so we can expect to see a more tightly regulated FDI landscape. Protected industries will extend from historically sensitive ones in defense and energy, to mundane ones such as food and drink, and more topical ones such as medicine and all data-rich sectors which cover just about everything. European nations are rapidly standing up their own versions of CIFIUS (the Committee on Foreign Investment in the United States), and legislators and policymakers are setting new clearance hurdles for investment, all of which will contain and constrain the free FDI flows of the past.

Double down on existing investment

Historically, greenfield investment accounted for half of all cross-border deals, but in part due to the pandemic restrictions, expansion and reinvestment projects from exiting investors has increased and many nations have adopted defensive policies and incentives for increased localization of enterprises.

Follow the money (not just projects)

The abundance of capital thanks to a decade of growth and the stymied demand forced on the global economy by the pandemic, meant that there is a deep river of cash flowing into private equity, funds IPOs, and M&A, which is globally mobile and driven by returns. Greenfield and expansion projects are too slow moving for these types of investor, and countries that make it easy for foreign funds to acquire or invest or indeed proactively promote investment portfolio opportunities in strategic industries (underwritten by government pledges) are likely to benefit considerably from this trend.

Authentic, inclusive and sustainable

People power though social media movements are forcing investors to confront environmental issues say in food packaging, fast fashion, and carbon intensive industries, and by association governments that are engaged with such companies as clients and host countries. Corporate social responsibility (CSR) is a hot potato issue in FDI today and likely to grow in importance. There has been a growing rejection of big global brands in favor of more local, authentic, and sustainable ones, from Budweiser to craft beer, Walmart to local independent farmers' markets, Hilton to Airbnb, and Amazon to the local independent record and bookstore revival. Big brands increasingly have to demonstrate the good that they are doing in the world, and this is certainly no less true in inward investment, which cannot be perceived to be exploitative, anti-competitive, or a threat to local enterprise. Another dimension of CSR is diversity and inclusion and locations that have intolerant or regressive social inclusion policies relating to gender, color, and ethnicity are unlikely to attract FDI in the new world order.

CFIUS is an interagency committee that can review mergers or other transactions that that could result in foreign control of a US business. They can advise the US president to suspend or prohibit any transaction deemed a threat to national security. Although it does not disclose the specific factors it takes into account, typically it will consider if the US business involved in the investment has links to US government agencies with national security responsibilities; involvement in critical technologies or products; or has offices or facilities in locations near sensitive government facilities (e.g. military bases, national laboratories, and others). Additionally, CFIUS will assess whether the transaction would result in foreign control over physical or virtual critical infrastructure.

The bot got my job

In terms of the future for IPAs, OCO undertook some research in late 2020/early 2021 among a sample of twenty-plus leading national IPAs from six continents to understand what innovation has taken place in terms of strategy, offer, processes, and technology/tools as a consequence of the pandemic or in response to the changing FDI outlook.

As a consequence, the pandemic response has brought many rather traditional and conservative government agencies screaming and shouting into the twenty-first century, and ways of working, response times, and use of sharing platforms have improved efficiencies and can only be for the benefit of the investor.

I believe there is still a long road to travel if investment agencies want to reach young, tech-rich talent and market-seeking firms, for whom the old model of investment promotion is just too slow and clunky. We live in a world where people can undertake customized research, compare options and prices, and effect transactions for a diverse range of products and services: homes, real estate, holidays, capital, supply chain, and consumer goods using sophisticated ecommerce marketplaces such as eBay, Alibaba, Trip Advisor, and Go Compare to mention just a handful. Here they can do benchmarking comparisons of factors that are most important to them and read reviews of previous clients and effect their transactions in a secure and regulated way.

I anticipate there will be a virtual marketplace for locations to promote their offers, and investors to browse and compare options/trade-offs and read unbiased reviews by previous investors. I am not suggesting that this will completely replace the role of investment promotion agencies, but it is likely to transform how they work, drive efficiencies around shortlisting, and open up the competition for a broader range of location options and clients, potentially funded and sponsored by relevant intermediaries such as lawyers, recruitment firms, relocation specialists, and real estate advisors.

In much the same way, the hotel business model has been transformed by the booking sites that allow them to reach a much wider universe of customers,

reduce reliance on channels such as agents, and facilitate dynamic pricing when demand surges or drops off. And as access to talent is rapidly becoming the most important variable in location choice for the most resilient sectors, there must be a link to talent mapping and recruitment for the most ambitious locations though this type of platform.

Clearly this digitally enabled approach to investment promotion will take care of a lot of volume, especially for market-seeking services and tech investments and facilitate self-service and light touch engagement with the investment promotion agency. This will free up resources for agency staff to focus on the more demanding, contestable, and high-impact investment, which needs access to sector expertise, regulators, and policymakers and needs a close relationship with government to pass regulatory hurdles.

If human capital and access to technology are the key drivers of FDI in the next decade, locations that can advance livability indicators such as affordable housing, diversity, tolerant social policies, progressive urban planning, low crime, accessible and affordable healthcare , high educational attainment, a clean/Green digitally enhanced business environment will be the destinations of the future.

And like all good hustles the FDI one is coming to an end. Inevitably technology levels the playing field, the hand of the regulator intervenes, the mugs get wiser, and the middlemen get side lined. And the politicians start telling the truth. And pigs might fly…..

Appendix

Printed in the United States
by Baker & Taylor Publisher Services